FRY'S TIES

STEPHEN FRY

FRY'S TIES

The Life and Times of a Tie Collection

Illustrations by Stephanie von Reiswitz
Photography by Clare Winfield

CHRONICLE BOOKS

SAN FRANCISCO

First published in the United States of America in 2023 by Chronicle Books.

Originally published in the United Kingdom in 2021 by Michael Joseph.

Text copyright © 2021 by Stephen Fry.
Photographs copyright © 2021 by Clare Winfield.
Illustrations copyright © 2021 by Stephanie von Reiswitz.

Pages 261–264 constitute a continuation of the copyright page.

Library of Congress Cataloging-in-Publication Data:

Names: Fry, Stephen, 1957- author. | Von Reiswitz, Stephanie, illustrator.
    | Winfield, Clare, photographer.
Title: Fry's ties : the life and times of a tie collection / Stephen Fry ;
    illustrations by Stephanie von Reiswitz ; photography by Clare Winfield.
Description: San Francisco : Chronicle Books, 2023. | "Originally published
    in the United Kingdom in 2021 by Michael Joseph."Identifiers: LCCN
2022059464 | ISBN 9781797221076 (hardcover)
Subjects: LCSH: Fry, Stephen, 1957- | Fry, Stephen, 1957---Clothing. | Neckties.
Classification: LCC PN2598.F79 A3 2023 | DDC 791.4502/8092 [B]--dc23/
eng/20230124
LC record available at https://lccn.loc.gov/2022059464

ISBN 978-1-7972-2107-6

Manufactured in China.

MIX
Paper | Supporting
responsible forestry
FSC
www.fsc.org   FSC™ C008047

Design by Maggie Edelman.

10 9 8 7 6 5 4 3 2 1

Chronicle books and gifts are available at special quantity discounts to corporations, professional associations, literacy programs, and other organizations. For details and discount information, please contact our premiums department at corporatesales@chroniclebooks.com or at 1-800-759-0190.

Chronicle Books LLC
680 Second Street
San Francisco, California 94107
www.chroniclebooks.com

CONTENTS

"CLOTHES MAKE THE MAN.
NAKED PEOPLE HAVE
LITTLE OR NO INFLUENCE
ON SOCIETY."

Mark Twain

TIES!

This all began back in March 2020. The public world had begun to shrink, but the domestic sphere was expanding in peculiar and unpredictable ways. With time and kitchen space on our hands, and yeast significantly less obtainable than marijuana or Yeezy footwear, proud photographs of homemade sourdough, flapjacks, and banana bread began to proliferate on social media streams. I was as guilty as anyone of contributing to this strange nuisance.

In other rooms, dust was being blown away, shelves artfully stocked for Zoom backgrounds, neglected cupboards excavated.

A week into lockdown, I found myself[1] sneezingly foraging in long-forsaken wardrobes and chests of drawers, in the course of which I uncovered drawerfuls of ties, bow ties, cravats, and scarves whose existence I had forgotten. Not forgotten, exactly—with prompting, I could have described them—but certainly abandoned and unthought of.

It came about that, on one of those tauntingly bright spring mornings when the forbidden outside world was all blossom and birdsong, I photographed a green silk necktie, composed a brief text on the subject of Façonnable, its maker, and posted the result on Instagram. Tens of thousands of likes and hundreds of replies and comments flew back, a response positive enough to encourage me to repeat the exercise the following day with another tie.

---

1   I use that formulation because so little that one did (found oneself doing) in those early days seemed to be propelled by any conscious act of will.

And so #fryties began.

More than a hundred ties later, on June 22 I wrote, "The days are getting longer now and the lockdown looser," and posted the final tie in the series. Many enthusiastic followers had been egging me to turn these posts into a book. Perhaps this was all part of the intensity (and boredom) of those early days of the pandemic. Now that I have actually gone ahead and produced such a book, those very same people might be thinking, "Steady on, Stephen. We didn't really *mean* it. A book of ties? Why the . . . What the . . . How the . . . I mean, *huh*?"

It may be (and as I write this *no one knows anything,* as my old friend William Goldman famously wrote—about Hollywood, but, boy, does it apply to the lockdown too) that there will be a very strong resistance to any books, films, or TV shows that go back to the worst days of the Covid-19 crisis. "As if we want to be reminded of *that,*" the general view might be. "Too soon, too soon."

Well, this book is about ties. Coronavirus might have instigated the project, but I hope it can stand on its merits as a book that ponders, speculates on, and celebrates ties.

But why *ties*?

OF TIES AND ME

Anyone can wear a tie. All you need is a neck, a shirt, and a feel for color.

Anyone can wear a tie, but few do. I am old enough to remember the time when the pavements of the City of London were populated by formidably formal figures perfectly arrayed in suit, collar, and tie. Not just a collar and a tie, but a *separate* collar and a tie. Most of you will be too young to remember that men of all classes wore shirts with separate collars right up to and into the 1960s. These were called "grandad shirts" by the girls and boys two generations below, who wore them without collars as amusing hand-me-downs. They made a good nightshirt too. Grandads themselves would only have been seen like that in their most relaxed moments. For work and Sunday best they would have affixed a collar (often heavily starched). This required a front and a back stud to anchor it all in place.

Both of my deceased grandfathers and a great-uncle had left collar boxes amongst the possessions that had come to us during my boyhood. These very adult and exotic objects intrigued and excited me, with their beautifully stamped monograms and their masculine aroma of camphor, bay rum, sandalwood, tobacco, and leather. The collars inside were in various styles: the usual pointed turndown collar; a variant with rounded ends; the wing (as worn by Neville Chamberlain); and the imperial, which went straight up but, unlike the wing collar, was not folded down into triangles at the ends—when properly worn, it forced the chin up high and gave one the air of a besashed and bemedaled European archduke.

As soon as I could, I took possession of these boxes (two circular and the other in a horseshoe shape) along with the collection of collarless shirts, silk and satin ties, starched collars, and metal and ivory collar studs[2] that accompanied them. I worked out, by tiresome trial and irksome error, the difference between a back stud and a front, and after many tears and curses became proficient in the art of dressing myself in the manner of two generations back. Rear stud first—*grunt*—then slip the tie in and round—*poke the tongue out to aid concentration*—fold the collar down—*don't crease it*—and finally, and most fiendishly, coordinate the thumb and fingers of both hands in such a way as to be able to insert the front stud without trapping the tie—*fierce stamping, sweating, and foul, foul language.*

Oh, it's a fiendish and fretful business, I assure you. That front stud has to be slipped through *four* different buttonholes—two at the collar ends, and two on the shirt where today there would be a top button—before getting a thumb or fingernail to close up the pivoting little disc at the rear. Vaguely similar to the business of doing up cuff links but twice as fiddly. If you managed it successfully, the tie would still be inside the collar, untwisted, and running free enough to be adjusted and tied. It was important to close the knot in such a way as to cover the stud. I still shake my head sorrowfully at period dramas on film and television today where the knot isn't done up fully and the stud (or, worse still, a *button*) is fully visible. Shoddy, I think to myself. Not done. Scarcely the ticket at all.

2 I'd like to think they were bone not ivory, but these were different times, for good and bad.

Which brings us on to the subject of *me*. What kind of teenager—in the fab and groovy 1960s as they whirled psychedelically into the '70s—would dress up in his grandfather's old togs and go into town sporting a shiny stiff collar and a silk or satin tie? A teenage Lord Snooty yearning to be beaten up by the Bash Street Kids, you might think. I suppose it did take a bit of courage on my part to dress quite so oddly, though I don't recall feeling especially brave. Perhaps I didn't care what people thought, an indifference to opinion that I have never since been able to recapture.

Here's the weird circle of youth and fashion. "Suits and ties are so yesterday," we declare. We have freed ourselves from convention and formality and now run about in jeans and T-shirts. But then this itself becomes a convention of its own, as parents *so* love to point out to their long-suffering children. "If you think that you're being more individual by dressing just like the rest of your generation . . ." And this leaves a space for the few who go backward rather than forward.

I am as certain as I can be that, had I been born forty years later than 1957, I would, as I grew into school age, have stood on the playground and sneered contemptuously at all those losers busy at their little screens sharing content from Instagram, Snapchat, and TikTok. How lame, I would have thought—probably out loud. I like to believe that I would have been most ostentatiously Off The Grid. "Sorry, sir, knowing your email address is no help. I don't have email. I can't deliver my homework that way. I don't have a printer. Or a laptop. Or a mobile phone. I can produce the essay on a typewriter, or using a fountain pen? I can slip it into your actual mailbox, in the sense of the slit in your front door. Any good to you?" My friends and I would have listened to our music on vinyl records and tape cassettes, communicated by landline telephones with dialing mechanisms and Bakelite brackets for cradles, exchanged messages by way of John le Carré one-time pads and dead letter drops, and probably produced a weird and provocative magazine using an old duplicator or mimeograph. In fuzzy type and on blue paper that would be hard for some digital doofus to scan or photocopy. And we would have thought ourselves the most excellently stylish kids in the world.

Well, born when I was, without ever perfecting stylishness I did mostly reject the fashions of my contemporaries and, where possible, exhibited myself in clothes of my grandfather's era, as described. I played 78 discs on a wind-up record player, listened to radio and music-hall comedians rather than prog-rock titans, and read Wodehouse, Waugh, Wilde, Chesterton, Dornford Yates, Dorothy Sayers, Henty, Kipling, Mary Renault, and Conan Doyle, and almost nothing by contemporary writers.

I may have been a lone weirdo as far as rural Norfolk and the medieval lanes of Norwich were concerned, but actually the Sgt. Pepper look, Chelsea bric-a-brac boutiques, and art-college groups like the Bonzo Dog Doo-Dah Band all told of the current retro fad for big-horned gramophones, bowler hats, the hussar and dragoon military swagger, ruched parasols, Kitchener mustaches, and all kinds of jumbled-up Edwardiana. My style then, if style it can be called, was a mixture of the bandstand, boater, and blazer nostalgia that slowly permeated Norfolk from London, and the world of aunts, valets, cads, loungers, and eccentric lords and ladies that I absorbed from my reading.

A big moment came in 1974 when the cinemas showed Jack Clayton's production of *The Great Gatsby*, with Robert Redford in the title role and Mia Farrow as a shimmeringly translucent Daisy Buchanan. I went nuts for Oxford-bag trousers, high V-neck sweaters, and piped blazers. As for those two-tone co-respondent shoes—*mwah*! My feet were already moving from size

12 to 13, but I squeezed myself into a pair of 11s and to hell with the pain and the pinching. By this time I was smoking ten or fifteen cigarettes a day. The everyday cheap British smokes—Embassy Regal, Player's No. 6, and Gold Sovereign—were nothing like good enough for me. It had to be Balkan Sobranie, Sobranie Cocktail, Sullivan Powell Private Stock, Fribourg & Treyer, or—if available—Passing Cloud.[3] These last, in their exquisite pink box lined with crisp tissue paper, were oval, which struck me as random and ridiculous at first, but I discovered that this flattened shape allowed them to fit into the slimmest of cigarette cases. Slim cigarette cases do not ruin the cut of a fellow's jacket. Or *coat*, one should say. To whip out a case, open it, and offer it to someone while murmuring, "Turkish this side, Virginia that"—life could afford no greater joy.

Yes, what a pretentious tosser, what a grade A tit. A lank-haired, lanky-limbed, lovelorn adolescent with stiff collar and bagged trouserings, parading with a cane[4] up Gentleman's Walk (Norwich's main shopping thoroughfare) and smoking unfiltered cigarettes

---

3   Fribourg & Treyer's elegant shop window in the Haymarket still stands, but the displays of exquisite cartons of gold-banded cigarettes and jars of snuff have long gone. On my rare trips to London as a teenager, I would go from Fribourg's to Sullivan Powell's in the Burlington Arcade, then over the road to St. James's, where Davidoff's, Dunhill's, and Astley's could be relied upon for fine pipe smokers' requisites and other arcane tobacco-related appurtenances, appliances, and accessories (reamers and cleaners, for example). Thence to the gloriously Dickensian Inderwick's on Carnaby Street and on to Smith's snuff shop on the Charing Cross Road. All of them, alas, now alive

4   I loved my silver-topped stick. But I soon lost it and had to make do with an umbrella from then on. Although, if you swing a brolly with the correct amount of restrained grace, it can still lend you the suave élan and debonair diablerie that are essential for a stylish promenade.

from a silver case—even sometimes through a tele-scopic holder, like some '20s flapper. At least I resisted wearing a monocle. I did happen upon one in a junk shop, but it kept falling out. Just wouldn't hold fast in the eye socket. I did affect a signet ring, though. And of course my desk drawer revealed even more evidence of an incipient young fogey. For my correspondence I used thick cream-colored "hand-laid" paper.[5] Scented violet ink. Sealing wax for the signet ring.

Oh Jesus, what a *wanker*.

It is a mercy that I wasn't beaten up. But Norwich-ites[6] are a tolerant bunch for the most part, and aside from a few mocking shouts in highfalutin toff tones—"Oh, I say, I say, I say. It's Lord Claude, don't you know!"—and assorted catcalls and raspberries, I was allowed to parade unmolested.

Now, I wouldn't want you to think that I was so assured, audacious, or authentic as to dress like this all the time. This was what you might call "a weak pose." A pose I could adopt and discard according to mood. There were many braver young people in the ranks of the goth, the proto-emo, and the punk, not to mention the pioneering outriders in the trans arena, inspired very often by Bowie, Bolan, and the so-called "gender benders" of the glam rock era. I was much more cowardly. An amateur without the guts to live the look through. I suppose I was what Pinter somewhere calls "a weekend wanker."[7] A paddler in the shallow end of self-exhibition. Some mornings I would dress like my brother and others of my age and class in straight-down-the-line jeans or cords under one of those brass-buttoned RAF greatcoats that were all

---

5   So it boasted. I was never quite sure what "hand-laid" meant, but it sounded pukka.

6   Should be "Norvicensians," I suppose.

7   The play *Old Times*, I think it is.

the rage. But on other mornings I would call for my invisible valet and desire him to lay out my finest prewar apparel.

I forbore to top these confections off with headgear of any kind. It was ties to which I gave my greatest attention. It had begun with the grand silk examples inherited from my grandfather, but even though I wasn't flush, I managed to find handfuls of affordable second- and thirdhand neckties, bow ties, and cravats at jumble sales and village fetes,[8] while strange rayon and Terylene specimens could be run to earth in charity shops and the grubbier kind of curiosity shop. By the time I was fifteen, I reckon I must have had more than forty ties. Nothing to what fills my drawers and cupboards today, but a good start.

8   Forerunners of the car boot and yard sales that are now so popular.

IF YOU WANT TO GET AHEAD, GET A HAT

Let us take a quick look at headgear for a moment.

I mentioned those gentlemen I saw in London's financial district in the mid-1960s. As a rule, they were outfitted in charcoal-colored three-piece suits and stiff collars, while some preferred a black jacket (or even a tailcoat) and striped trousers. But what would make such figures stand out in any street today is that they almost all wore bowler hats. They really did. The bowler had been a symbol of Britishness for many decades. All the world, and every cartoonist and TV comedy producer, knew that American men were clean-shaven, wore Hawaiian shirts, stuck fat cigars between their teeth, and had shiny cameras slung around their necks. Frenchmen were furiously mustachioed, wore berets and striped jerseys, and had strings of onions slung around their necks. British men were more discreetly mustached, wore bowler hats, carried neatly furled umbrellas, and had school, regimental, or club ties around their necks. Think Thomson and Thompson in *Tintin*, or Frank Dickens's comic-strip office worker Bristow.

Thanks to the paintings of René Magritte and that scene in the Pierce Brosnan remake of *The Thomas Crown Affair*, there is a faintly surreal quality to all those bowler hats bobbing along the pavements. And sprinkled amongst them, I remember, men in *top* hats could also be seen. Bowlers and toppers. The top-hatted ones were perhaps special kinds of City beadle or warden. Years later, when I went to university, I got very used to the sight of college porters and proctors in bowler or top hats, the style varying from college to college. But the point is that, even in my lifetime (and I do persist in thinking of myself as belonging to the modern age, for all my peculiarities), Men Wore Hats.

I recall once—in about 1964, when I was six or seven—walking with my mother along Whitehall. As we moved in the direction of Trafalgar Square, she pointed up at the Cenotaph and told me that men always raised or tipped their hats when passing it. I snorted with disbelieving scorn, as children do. I stopped to watch and prove her wrong. But bless me, sure enough, each hatted man that passed by did indeed raise his hat, or at the least put a quick finger to its brim, mostly without even turning his head in the Cenotaph's direction. A reflex, everyday action. I have never doubted my mother since.[9]

My memory doesn't play me false. The world truly was highly hatted when I was young. Watch film footage from any time until the mid-1960s and you will see men from every walk of life whose heads exhibit a bewildering assortment of homburgs, fedoras, trilbies, caps, boaters, bowlers, and berets, while the women present an array of cloches, picture hats, pillboxes, and

---

9   Fact.

other species of millinery whose proper names I shall never know.

What I've described is very white, male, and preposterous, of course. Which is why it needed the boot up its backside administered by the youth explosion and countercultural excitements that were already rumbling below the surface the afternoon Mother and I walked up Whitehall. That summer, my birthday treat was a trip to the cinema to see the first Beatles film, *A Hard Day's Night*. The world was ripe for change.

Old enough to have ridden on steam trains, to have been flogged by schoolmasters for almost any act of disobedience or display of impertinence, to have lived in a world where the daily milk was delivered in horse-drawn floats, and to have been turned away from restaurants for not wearing a tie. Yet young enough to have watched all that disappear.[10]

---

10 There are grand five-star hotels where a tie was obligatory until very recently, but the need to attract the patronage and custom of music and movie stars, baseball-capped and T-shirted Hollywood producers and playwear Silicon Valley billionaires has more or less put an end to all that. Private clubs still insist on a tie, but there aren't many establishments open to the general public that do.

THE DEATH OF THE TIE?

Like bowler hats, ties were beginning to be seen as tokens of Form and Formality, outdated and irrelevant, a reminder of the stifling conformity of unhappier times.

For millions of people—men and boys mostly, but of course not exclusively—ties were something that *had* to be worn. As school uniform, in church, for lunch with aunts and uncles in a grand (or would-be grand) hotel, for certain kinds of grown-up parties, for funerals, and later . . . yuck . . . for job interviews. If that interview bore fruit, some kind of tie became everyday office wear; salesman wear; junior, middle, and senior management wear; executive wear. Politicians, policemen, soldiers, lawyers, doctors, teachers . . . members of all the professions wore ties. Taking a tie *off* rapidly became a symbol of downtime, me time, relaxing-with-a-whiskey-and-soda time. Daddy's home! Off with the tie, on with the cardie, pipe, and slippers. Ooh! Look at Nick Clegg, Rishi Sunak, and Tony Blair—they've loosened their ties and taken off their jackets. Why, they're just like us!

Ties were seen by some to be well named—they tied you up and tied you down. Ties were associated with authority, convention, maleness if not masculinity, and an unquestioning acceptance of the straight rails on which your life was supposed to run. In the 1950s and '60s the mods and teds made what they could of slim, jazzy ties in rayon and satin, and the late-flourishing kipper tie enjoyed a brief and cheerful time in the sun, but rebellion against ties became the natural posture of any self-respecting youth. "Do I *have* to wear this bloody thing?" "I can't breathe in it." "It won't tie." "No one else is wearing them." These were the adolescent moans heard around the world. If a tie absolutely *had* to be worn, then the very least the sullen teenager could do was to loosen the top shirt button behind its knot, to show that the object was being worn reluctantly and that a living, breathing rebel, yearning to break free, was smoldering behind it. There was even a fad for wearing them around the head in a Keith Richards manner, or making ironic punk use of them, along with gray shorts and snake belts.

Alex "Hurricane" Higgins, the mesmerizingly charismatic wild child of '70s snooker, finagled a doctor's order that allowed him to jettison the bow tie decreed by snooker's governing body. Smart dress was supposed to show how far the game had come from the smoke and booze of rough working-men's clubs and unsavory billiard halls. But the more rebellious, cool, roguish, watchable, and popular players—men like Higgins and Jimmy White—earned the people's love precisely because they never pretended to aspire to middle-class respectability.

Around this time, Hollywood (and its audience) was undergoing profound change: The bolo and slim tie of early Newman and McQueen faded out along with the trilby and fedora that had ruled since Cagney and Bogart days.

Farther up the Californian coast, a new kind of figure was emerging in a new kind of industry. Steve Jobs never wore a tie. Apple employees were *allowed* to, of course—"Hey, no rules here"—but none did. Ties were for the sad staffers of Big Blue, the nickname given to IBM on account of the dark-navy suits that the corporation's employees had to wear—along with a tie, of course. Later on, when IBM's threat faded and Microsoft became their major rival, Apple put out a series of commercials comparing the PC to the Mac. The actor Justin Long, representing the Mac, wore a stylish jersey, jeans, and sneakers. John Hodgman, as the PC, wore a suit or jacket, and always a tie. Apple was trying to position the Mac as the computer of choice for those who were not throttled by the rules of convention, those who (in their grammatically challenging advertising strapline) "think different"—different from the suffocated, strangulated, tight-arsed, tight-throated, emotionally constipated, corporate, gray, beige, boring people of the *business* world. The Silicon Valley pioneers who gave us Google, YouTube, Amazon, Uber, Twitter, and Facebook called their headquarters "campuses," and crammed them with primary-colored play areas, meditation pods, slides, swings, sleeping nests, and climbing walls—Fisher-Price activity mats scaled up for adults, or at least for what now passed for adults.

And these companies rapidly became the most valuable businesses on earth. In the Great Disruption[11] there wasn't time to respond, consider, and act in a manner that was mature, slow, reflective, uncertain, and generally Grown Up. That sort of thing went with the kind of people who wore ties. Their day was over and the world belonged to the young, the audacious, and the fiercely casual.

One of the last bastions of tie wearing had been the world of finance. But even on Wall Street and in the City seismic changes could be felt. There was a great deal of moving fast and breaking things in this sector too. There was the "Big Bang" in Thatcher's Britain—a series of deregulations that included the privatization

---

11 "Move fast and break things" was Facebook's proud slogan, and one they lived up to. They are now moving much more slowly to mend things.

of previously publicly owned corporations and utilities, and a system-wide loosening of shackles, which offered irresistible incentives to take risks and invent new and ever more complex financial ploys, dodges, and "instruments." Derivatives, hedge funds, zero-coupon bonds, SPACs, short positions, and . . . Even as I write these terms down, I am forced to confess that I could live to sixty and never understand them. Oh, I *am* sixty. Over sixty . . . and . . . it turns out I was right, I don't understand them. The decades pass, game theory and staggeringly complex and "creative" mathematical models allow even more extraordinary opportunities to make money in the markets. Until it all collapses, that is.

The Wolves of Wall Street or Masters of the Universe, or whatever pathetically self-regarding title they gave themselves or were given by their sycophantic adherents, mostly wore ties. But they loosened them by lunchtime at the latest, and had removed them entirely by the cocktail and cocaine hour. An hour that moved backward toward lunch with irrepressible momentum. So, yes, they did wear ties—but in a way that said, "We play squash. We party hard. We're from the wrong side of the tracks. We march to a different drum. The rule book has been thrown out of the window. These are ties, yeah, but they are Fuck-You Ties."

In the public-facing worlds of broadcasting and politics, as in so many other spheres of human behavior, things are turned upside down so far as ties are concerned. What was respectable yesterday is repressive and despicable today. Imagine a presenter of *The One Show* or the host of an afternoon quiz daring to appear in a tie. Inconceivable. Here is the opening of a news story taken from the *Guardian* in 2012:

J eremy Paxman has made history by appearing on *Newsnight* this week without a tie. Traditionally, male news presenters across all television channels wear ties, because it conveys the necessary air of authority and respectability that viewers might expect when receiving serious information. But Paxman is a maverick who plays by his own rules; it's worth noting that he went one step further than just ditching his neckwear, by leaving not one but two buttons undone on his shirt. Did he think he could revolutionise television protocol in one fell swoop? Probably, because that's the kind of chap he is.

In 2007, Paxman wrote on the BBC website: "Is it time for *Newsnight* men to stop wearing ties? It has always been an utterly useless part of the male wardrobe. But now, it seems to me, the only people who wear the things daily are male politicians, the male reporters who interview them—and dodgy estate agents." Yet it has taken him five years to put his money where his mouth is, so he clearly has felt duty bound to follow the rules of his profession—until now. Politicians like to bury bad news stories about their party when a huge global disaster suddenly dominates the media, releasing them at a carefully chosen time. Perhaps Paxman used the BBC's current huge PR disaster to bury his hated collection of ties?

Ties have not entirely disappeared from our television screens, of course. I was able to get away with wearing them when presenting the BBC program *QI* because they were arty, unusual, and so carefully chosen (by the production's wardrobe designer mostly, only occasionally by me) as to be a semicomical *feature*.

Jon Snow anchored *Channel 4 News* for decades and his "signature" ties were a feature too. Jools Holland's gray three-piece suits and his ties are part of his timeless "Mr. Music" look. Men who want to be taken seriously must be open-collared when hosting quizzes, game shows, talk shows, news discussion programs . . . To wear a tie is to be out of touch.

In a generation and a half, the tie has moved from being a sign of respect to a sign of snobbish self-satisfied distance from the common run of humanity. And politicians (perhaps heeding Paxman) can't wait to ditch their jackets and ties at the first opportunity to show how down with the ordinary folks they are. I wrote the following about Governor Mitt Romney in 2008, after a day spent following him on the presidential campaign trail for a BBC documentary:

With a great flurry of handshakes and smiles Mitt is suddenly in the house, marching straight to the space in front of the fireplace where a mike on a stand awaits him, as for a stand-up comedian. He is wearing a smart suit, the purpose of which, it seems, is to allow him to whip off the jacket in a moment of wild unscripted anarchy, so as to demonstrate his informality and desire to get right down to business and to hell with the outrage and horror this will cause in his minders. British MPs and candidates of all stripes now do the same thing. The world over, male politicians have trousers that wear out three times more quickly than their coats. And who would vote for a man who kept his jacket on? Why, it is tantamount to broadcasting your contempt for the masses. Politicians who wear jackets might as well eat the common people's children and have done with it.

After that glad-handing session was over, he was back on the road:

> noticed that the Governor's jacket had somehow magically been placed in the back of his SUV. Ready to be put on in order to be taken off again next time.

Things have moved on even since Paxman's broadside. Ties are now not even for male politicians. Ties are dead.

Unless—and it's an "unless" that swings wide a great portal of possibilities—unless, that is, ties appeal to you in and of themselves. Not as tokens of this or emblems of that, but as miniature theaters in which compact dramas of design, form, color, and meaning can be played out on a triangular stage small enough to be discreet, but open and available enough to be appreciated by those with an eye or an urge to look.

Why the tie for such displays? Well, shirts, jackets, and suits that come as intricately patterned and excitedly colored as ties make much bolder and more conspicuous statements, and while there are plenty of people flamboyant and confident enough to go about under such eye-catching canvases, I can't be counted amongst them. If every day is ripe for party dress, don't real parties become something of a letdown?

What else can one wear that allows one to murmur—but not shout—one's love of design, form, patterning, and color? Red, yellow, green, and blue trousers might be considered acceptable in the Cotswolds, but please may they stay there and never escape. Socks can delight with jazzy patterns and crazy colorways, but we don't really go about the place gazing at one another's ankles. A flash of bravura clocking at the heel might reveal itself when giving a hitch before seating, or when crossing the legs, but no ... For me the tie is the Goldilocks of exhibition spaces. Not too hot and not too cold. Not too big and not too small. Just right. A little pop of color, as designers like to say, a micro work of art that can be ignored or admired, that proclaims neither the introvert nor the extrovert.

BACK
TO ME

In 1977, as the tide of glam rock began to swell and the first pustular pimples of proto-punk began to break out, I was still parading around London in stiff collar and silk tie, still smoking Sobranie Cocktails, still an insufferable prick, but now also a wanted criminal. I shan't go into details, they are unfolded elsewhere,[12] but once I had emerged from prison and found myself at last a university student, the old desire to dress like a '20s mannequin had vanished like mist in the wind. I was determined to behave properly and not let my parents down ever again. I had sown my wild oats and now it was time to grow sage, as someone once said, almost wittily.

Harris Tweed jacket, dark-green or Prussian-blue moleskin trousers, brown brogues,[13] a cotton shirt, and a pleasing tie: This, I thought, was the proper rig-out for an earnest and diligent undergraduate. For the first week I made the horrifying mistake of wearing a *college* tie, but once it had become apparent that this was an unpardonable floater I replaced it with quietly authoritative specimens: small gold dots on a maroon or emerald ground, that sort of thing. More English

---

12 I can scarcely recommend *Moab Is My Washpot* highly enough. Available wherever you source your criminal memoirs.

13 Though I did have a pair of olive-green Kickers that I loved with a great passion.

market town than French or Italian metropolis. For one thing, I couldn't afford the fashionable confections; for another, my tastes then did run to the domestic more than to the continental. So far as neckjoy was concerned, I wanted MGs, Wolseleys, and Bristols, supplemented by the rare treat of an E-Type or an Aston Martin. Ferraris, Maseratis, and Lamborghinis were just not my style. I don't remember wearing a *bow* tie, I am happy to say. Perhaps I tried once and then looked at the few other students who did sport them and decided that I had no wish to be bracketed with *them*, thank you very much.

The late '70s and early '80s were times when the practice of bracketing, siloing, sandlotting, ghettoizing, taxonomizing, categorizing, and balkanizing was really starting to become a Thing. Acronyms and epithets like "yuppie" and "Sloane Ranger" were beginning to be giggled over in the columns of glossy magazines, from which it is always a short hop to the broadsheets and at last the tabloids and the wider public consciousness. In today's world of Identity this has all gone much, much further, of course. As "millennials," "Gen Z," and "boomers," we are further splintered into a confounding cascade of social, cultural, sexual, political, and other subgenres. Martin Luther King Jr., who exhorted that we should judge people only by "the content of their character," might be baffled and, one assumes, hurt by how much *all* of us (nonracist, progressive, and kindly disposed as we might imagine ourselves to be) are now in thrall to labeling and to the many kinds of prejudice, bias, and (frankly) bigotry that result from such labeling. The basis of our judgments has nothing to do with MLK's ideal of character content, but everything to do with circumstances of birth, upbringing, accent, taste, ethnicity, fashion, belonging, and *identity*. I would not claim that this has never been seen before in human history. Such sifting and indexing and filing goes back to the dawn of writing. Aristophanes,

Menippus, and the Roman satirists were adept at laughing at *types*.

Some forms of dress are clearly deliberate statements, if not of identity, then of loyalty and kinship. A teenager in a death metal T-shirt wants the world to know what their taste in music is. But you don't need to have lived very long amongst humans to know that such outward presentations of preference are no sure guide to character, nature, or disposition. When I was first nervously poking my nose into the gay "scene" in London, it was quickly made apparent that the frighteningly dressed clubbers in chains, leather, studs, muscle vests, and similar butch bondage paraphernalia were very often a great deal sweeter, warmer, shyer, and friendlier than the angel-faced twinks who draped themselves around the place looking as if butter wouldn't melt in their . . . in any part of them. But the mistake would be to make that itself a rule, of course. To say that all S&M-togged macho men are darlings and all honey-sweet youths are sour bitches is as silly, lazy, and wrong as insisting on the opposite.

Why am I telling you this? You know it. Book, cover, judge, don't. We all know it, but I have yet to meet anyone who isn't quite as guilty as I can be of making confident character appraisals on the basis of appearance, class, adherence, or other accidents of birth and upbringing. Even on the basis of something so apparently insignificant as a tie.

We can tell ourselves that tie-wearers believe themselves superior in tone, education, style, and importance, just because they are wearing a tie. But while we are thinking that, the tie-wearers may be telling themselves that the world looks on them as pompous, old-fashioned, unadventurous, and boring, just because they are wearing a tie.

In this sense we can allow ties to stand as representative of our constant reading and misreading of the signs, symbols, ciphers, tokens, emblems, and badges that surround and assail us in the human world.

"It's loose around the collar; the top button is undone. The bloody thing's too short and frayed at the end. I'm supposed to wear it to work. Who cares? I'm not to be constricted by rules, codes, and protocols." So one wearer seems to be saying.

Another wearer seems to be saying, "It is black with a thin blue stripe. If you know, you know. That's right, I went to Eton. Deal with that as you wish."

Yet another: "All right, I have to wear a tie for work. I'm an accountant. I know you think accountancy's boring, but look. This wild designer swirl of color should tell you there's more to me than meets the eye."

"Please notice me."

"Please don't notice me."

There is, too, what you might call the rhythm of the wearing.

"He has worn that same tie every day this week."[14]

"Every time I see them, they're wearing a completely different and clearly expensive tie."

"Oh, a half-Windsor today, I see?"

---

14 A kind of cult don at Cambridge, Jeremy Prynne, a
    fellow of Caius College, lecturer, and "open field" poet,
    now retired from teaching, always wore the same orange
    tie (or, at least, identical orange ties) for the decades
    in which he delivered his celebrated lectures on poetry.
    Rarely seen without it.

Once you have excluded the obvious messages—very chic silk Italian, retro mod, swanky regiment, Oxbridge college, exclusive club, '50s spiv, cowboy, country doctor, racecourse cad—most ties are, it must be admitted, as ordinary and unnoticeable (or unworthy of notice) as socks. Sometimes a tie is a tie is a tie and there's little or nothing to read.

But for those who think there is such a thing as "overreading," and that close analysis and detailed deconstructions are pretentious, try for a moment to think of a corner of fashion like the tie as being similar to a corner of rural Britain. Let's say, a field in Bedfordshire. Can you *overread* a field? There's agronomical, agricultural, riparian, chemical, biological, zoological, mineralogical, and geological data encoded into every sod, furrow, and stile. And that is before we start on the cultural, historical, aesthetic, and romantic qualities of the countryside. You can't *overread* a field in Bedfordshire. And you can't, I would urge you to believe, overread a tie.

Having said which,[15] I am not going full in on French semiotics. Roland Barthes could have written a marvelous essay on the meaning of ties. I neither have the intellectual capacity nor the wish to drill down so deep, but I hope in the following pages you'll share with me a sense that the tie is nonetheless a rich and fascinating field for designers, for wearers, and for those with an eye to social fads, fancies, and fluctuations.[16]

---

15 My friend Hugh has pointed out that Havingsaidwhich is a village in the Cotswolds. Perhaps it's twinned with Albeit in Nottinghamshire and the Welsh hamlet of Heretofore.

16 I know my habit of alliteration is maddening. I'm so sorry. A leopard can't lange his lots.

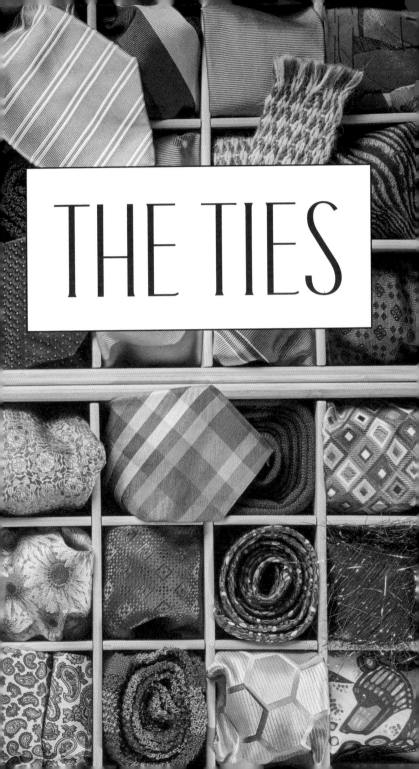

THE TIES

If you know me, you might well be aware of my love of the mythology, art, drama, and architecture of ancient Greece. So you won't be surprised that I own a tie like this. It's sadly unworn; I think I was saving it up for a party yet to take place.

Books could be written about this tie. One might be on the subject of the city of Athens and its mythical origins, and on the Panathenaic Games, whose rituals and processions are carved on the marble frieze of the Parthenon and are what this tie depicts. Another book would be on the injustice of the British Museum, to this day refusing to return to their rightful place the Parthenon marbles taken by Lord Elgin nearly 220 years ago. There is no credible or honorable case for the BM freezing onto the frieze. The marbles could be cast first so that exact replicas would still stand in the museum, alongside a "Parthenon Experience" in which the visitor could watch how they were packed up, transported, and installed in their proper places in the New Acropolis Museum in Athens. What a classy act it would be on their part to return them!

One or two of you might have noted that this tie is black and white. Of course one of the reasons this tie is essentially monochrome is because the last of the paint that would have decorated the original frieze was cleaned off by scholars, who believed the marble should be gleaming white.

A ha—a glimpse of my good old "egg and bacon." The tie of the Marylebone Cricket Club. Plenty of you are already snorting, yawning, fidgeting, sneering, or shaking your head in bewilderment. But others will know whereof I speak. A twenty-nine-year waiting list for membership gives you some idea that membership in the MCC is certainly highly prized, weird and preposterous as that may seem to many. It gives one access to parts of the Lord's Cricket Ground that are as hallowed as religious shrines. The Long Room, the Committee Room . . . the little aeries and secret places from which to watch the cricket. Pavilioned in splendor and girded with praise, as the old hymn has it.

I am old enough to know that you cannot make someone like cricket any more than you can make them like Wagner. We lovers of these things are used to having to apologize and bow our heads while we are told how boring such pursuits are. Well, they each in their own way give me deeper and more abiding pleasure than most things in life, and if that makes me a sucker, or a poseur, or something else unacceptable— well, so be it.

I think that, unlike the Garrick Club's "salmon and cucumber" tie, which can be sported anywhere, it is rather frowned upon to wear the MCC's "egg and bacon" anywhere other than at Lord's. To wear it to a match at the Oval or Headingley, for example, would surely be the height of bad form. Members can obtain the tie from the MCC shop at Lord's, but Dege & Skinner are one of the few family-owned Savile Row tailors left, so they are worth supporting.

A little anecdote about the Lord's Committee Room, if I may. E. W. "Jim" Swanton, veteran cricket writer, once came out of the Committee Room saying, in shocked tones, "There's a *woman* in there!" "Yes, Jim. It's the Queen; she's visiting." A long pause, and then one word from Jim. "Nevertheless . . ." Happily, that sort of thing has changed . . .

Beverly Hills' Rodeo Drive. Singapore's Orchard Road. Fifth Avenue, New York. Avenue Montaigne, Paris. Via Monte Napoleone, Milan. London's . . . Jermyn Street?

I know, I know. Why wouldn't I write "Bond Street," or even "Oxford Street"? Both are better known. And yet, Jermyn Street is a significant player in the world of *Fry's Ties*. This quiet, unassuming thoroughfare has been the spiritual home of British neckties (and menswear) for the better part of three hundred years, and we will be strolling down this sacred street many times during the course of this book.

Jermyn Street (or "Jarman Streete," as it was first recorded) takes its name from Henry Jermyn, Earl of St. Albans (1605–84). A courtier and politician, Henry was not an overly popular member of the Stuart court. He did, however, have one very influential friend and confidante—Henrietta Maria de Bourbon, wife of Charles I. Indeed, rumors circulated that Henry was the real father of Charles II. After helping restore Charles II to the throne, Henry was leased a parcel of land north of St. James's Palace in 1661.

An admirer of the classical revival sweeping Europe, the earl helped popularize the architectural style in England. Rather than the timber-framed houses and unpaved streets typically seen in the capital before the Great Fire, Henry planned elegant stone-faced buildings surrounded by broad paved streets. Fourteen grand townhouses and four new streets—including one named after himself—were built for aristocratic households. The area's proximity to St. James's Palace and the royal park meant that luxury merchants quickly followed, eager to sell their wares to the great and the good. Wine, cheese, perfume, boots, and eventually neckwear—Jermyn Street became *the* destination for a nineteenth-century gentleman.

On April 17, 1941, at around 3 a.m., a Luftwaffe parachute mine exploded on Jermyn Street. The area was badly damaged, with many lives lost. The night of April 16–17, 1941, was, in fact, one of the worst of the war. It became known, simply, as "The Wednesday."

History, cheese, ties—I hope you'll agree that Jermyn Street deserves its place on my list.

The statue of the great Regency dandy Beau Brummell gazes down on New & Lingwood's double premises at the Jermyn Street end of the Piccadilly Arcade. The words on the label of this particular tie might be enough to make many of you retch with furious contempt. "London, Eton, Cambridge." Yes, "New & Lingwood, Shirtmakers and Hosiers" certainly do give off an aroma of Old Establishment. St. James's, public school, and Oxbridge—what could be more loathsome to modern sensibilities? But hold off awhile. At a time when every high street in the world carries the same international "luxury" brands, an independent British company composed of magnificently talented makers is surely more to be celebrated than decried. No? No? Oh, okay then. They make jackets, suits, shirts, and the most astoundingly beautiful dressing gowns I've ever seen.*

Whebodyn I was younger and even sillier than I am now, I used to pride myself on being able to tell the individual make of a Jermyn Street shirt, just from the cut and lie of the collar. Turnbull & Asser, Harvie & Hudson, New & Lingwood, Hawes & Curtis, Hilditch & Key, T.M. Lewin, Charles Tyrwhitt—they all had their own individual style. New & Lingwood's shirts were my favorite on account of the shallow angle of the collar tabs. Turnbull & Asser's were good but more acute, which made the knot of the tie sit less elegantly, in my view at least.

I went into New & Lingwood to buy a tie as a Christmas present for someone a few years back and fell into conversation with the young fellow who was boxing the goods up and doing the gift wrapping. He said that his friends thought he had the lamest Christmas job possible. I said he could tell everyone that actually he was a professional tie-boxer (Thai boxer, geddit?!).

* No, I'm not being paid,
  or sponsored, or offered
  any freebies. Honestly,
  the cynicism . . . !

Versace is not really to my taste, if I'm honest. But back in the mid-1980s, I spent a fair amount of time in New York City. A new production of the musical *Me and My Girl* had opened on Broadway, and I was responsible for the "book"—musical-theater jargon for the plot, dialogue, and other non-song-and-dance elements. It became, improbably, quite a hit.

I loved strolling up and down the Upper East Side so much that I eventually bought an apartment in that neighborhood. One would often see Andy Warhol and a small entourage going in and out of the stores there. One morning I thought I'd follow him into one of them. Arsey thing to do, but I thought, "He is Andy Warhol . . ." So when he entered Gianni Versace I went in after him. He fell into conversation with the manager. Or maybe it was a member of the Versace family. I was instantly approached by a rather forbidding henchman, so I panicked and bought a tie. It might have been this one or another, a nautical yellow, blue, and white striped tie.

I do have a third Gianni V somewhere, with a lion on it. Lions, Greek keys, Roman grandeur in yellow and gold . . . No, not my kind of thing at all, really. But many love the style.

Christian Lacroix certainly makes a handsome tie. I do have a shot of m'colleague and me from the third series of our TV show *A Bit of Fry & Laurie*, for which the BBC lavished three ties on each of us. Two of mine were from Lacroix. The floral motif on this particular tie is a daisy. The daisy, as some of you might know, was sacred to the ancient Germanic goddess of spring and the dawn from whom (if we believe our Bede) Easter takes its name. What with "Lacroix" being French for "the cross" and all, the name is a remarkably appropriate one to bandy about on Good Friday. Henceforth this shall be known as my Easter tie.

"I was after a pair of shoes."

"Ah very well. I shall
serve them first."

"No, no. I meant I am looking
for a pair of shoes."

"To buy?"

"To buy."

"Mr. Dalliard. The gentleman
wishes to buy a pair of shoes . . .
Oh, what rotten decomposing
luck. Mr. Dalliard tells me we
have no shoes."

This image, in which I wear the delightful Lacroix tie, is, of
course, from a different *A Bit of Fry & Laurie* episode. But I
couldn't resist.

"How dull," you might yawn. "This tie is the plainest thing we've ever seen."

Dull it might look, but the eyes of those who know these kinds of things will have lit up at once. A Household Division tie. The Life Guards and the Blues and Royals are cavalry, while the Grenadier, Coldstream, Scots, Irish, and Welsh Guards make up the infantry regiments. I used to know them by the arrangement of buttons on their red coats; it was a schoolboy thing back then.

Surprisingly, perhaps, it's much "smarter" to be in the infantry than the cavalry. Lord Randolph, Winston Churchill's father, was disgusted that his son's career at Sandhurst was so poor that he could "only" get into a mounted regiment. Mind you, it did allow the history-hungry young Churchill to take part in one of the last British cavalry charges, at the Battle of Omdurman, in the Sudan, in 1898. Anyway, on my occasional forays

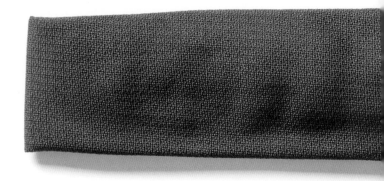

into the palaces of the mighty I have noticed that at least three out of five royal equerries will sport this tie.

The stripes on British "rep" ties (where the stripes signify a regiment, corps, college, club, school, etc.) angle down from the left shoulder, or "from heart to right hand," as they say. American rep ties tend to go from the right shoulder down toward the left hip. Something to watch out for.

Look. I know the coded complexities and exclusive eccentricities of the British Establishment are disgraceful, fusty, and absurd, but at least I found an appropriate use for this tie. I have no right to it, of course. I must have been given it to wear for filming when playing some oily spy chief or something—my usual kind of role. I wore it most recently for a little sketch on the BBC in which I played a descendant of the Melchett family, long servants of the Crown.

Ah, a classic paisley on cream. My favorite of the bunch, the tie on the bottom left, is from Zenith. The name "Cernobbio" on the brand's label betrays the tie's origins—the glorious Lake Como in northern Italy. It was here in the late 1400s that, as tradition has it, Ludovico Sforza, the Duke of Milan (an ancestor of Shakespeare's Prospero, perhaps), decreed mulberry trees should be planted to encourage the rearing of *Bombyx mori*, the silkworm, and the weaving of its glistening fiber.

Years earlier, Marco Polo had returned from his travels to China with bolts of this magical textile and tales of its production. The nearest city to Como is, of course, Milan—which, over the centuries, in part thanks to the silk from Como and Cernobbio, became (and still remains) Italy's fashion capital.

I think there is something very pleasing about the horizontal cording effect in the weave of this tie. There is a Zenith in India that makes ties too, in case the name struck a different chord with you, but they are unrelated.

THE HALF-WINDSOR KNOT

For those of you who abominate sport, who are bored or irritated by it, apologies. But ties reflect just about all human life—athletic and ludic competition not excluded.

A little while ago, I had the honor to be on the board of Norwich City Football Club for five years. My poor attendance and general hopelessness in committee meant that the time came to agree that a role as a kind of ambassador, friend, and social media poster on behalf of the Canaries would suit me better than sitting around a table gazing with dumb incomprehension at spreadsheets and financial reports. A place in the Directors' Box is a very obvious perk of board membership, and with it, for males, comes the requirement to present yourself in jacket and tie. It's tradition to sport a tie in club colors on such occasions—either shop-bought or from the official club store.

h, Nicole Miller. Hard to believe just how hip, hot, and happening her neckwear was back in the mid to late 1980s. These were the yuppie ties par excellence. Every time I visited New York I'd hare off to one of her stores on Madison Avenue in search of the latest designs. She added boxer shorts too. Nicole Miller is still going as a designer, I believe, but for women only—no longer decorating men's collars with her wildly bold designs. A good thing, you may think. I don't know. Restrained taste has its place, but sometimes a dash of vigor and silliness can cheer one up, no?

"WHAT DO TIES MATTER, JEEVES, AT A TIME LIKE THIS?"

"THERE IS NO TIME, SIR, AT WHICH TIES DO NOT MATTER."

P. G. Wodehouse

Ties are worn for all kinds of reasons—club ties, regimental ties, and *work* ties. There are such things. Ties designed by or for an employer, to be worn by members of its staff. Many, many years ago, between A levels and university, when all around here was green fields, I worked for a short while at the department store Bonds of Norwich.

Bonds is a John Lewis now, but it was not unlike Grace Brothers in *Are You Being Served?* in many ways. Mr. Eric and Mr. Richard were the two Bond family members who patrolled the departments—a little younger than the sprightly valetudinarian Young Mr. Grace, but with a very similar air of benign patriarchal amiability. The shop's symbol was a bee.

I started in Homewares but was moved up to Furniture on the top floor, for which I had to wear a dark suit and this splendid tie. Furniture's Mr. Ellis (a marvelous man who introduced me to the writings of Malcolm Lowry) and I would patrol the floor, trying to get customers interested in our lines of Ercol furniture. I would say things like, "Madam certainly has an eye. She has instinctively picked out the finest dining table in Norwich." Or, "Surely the question Sir should be asking is, 'Can Sir afford *not* to own so exquisite a sofa?'" Later I was moved to Dispatch and would ride shotgun on the delivery vans.

Dear old Bonds. It never felt like work.

I don't think I've ever met Johnnie Boden, and I'm sure he's a lovely fellow, but his CV is the kind that makes many shiver with rage, revulsion, resentment, or ridicule. Eton, Oxford, Warburg's investment bank in the City, a spot of stockbroking, and then—good-oh!— he receives an inheritance from an uncle and starts up a clothing catalog company and makes himself a massive fortune. Artful leisurewear for men who favor loafers without socks in their Oxfordshire weekend houses; charming prints for women; adorable sun bonnets for infants. Boden evokes a lifestyle skillfully reinforced by the backgrounds in their catalog photographs: good gardens, a solid but fun and unpompous country look. Buy into it and you feel you could be your own Monty Don in your own Longmeadow, with your own Guernsey sweaters and your own retrievers.

Yes, Boden is easy to sneer at, but easy to look upon wistfully too. There are dark things in the world more worth getting cross at than the Boden catalog, after all; truly, flicking through it and ordering from it doesn't

make you a bad person. The company does stop short of red trousers and panama hats, at least for men. If you want the Michael Portillo pistachio linen jacket look, you'll have to go elsewhere.

When I found this tie at the back of a drawer some time ago, my heart skipped a beat. I fell on it with a glad cry. "This is a good one," I thought to myself. "Is it Christian Lacroix? Lanvin? What?" When I turned it over and saw the label, I was very surprised. Given Boden's cunningly relaxed signature look, any formal neck-wear at all seems so unlikely. I thought at first I must have ordered it from the catalog myself, but my mother thinks that she perhaps gave it to me as a birthday present. It was cheerful, a quality she much prizes. As do I. My sister believes quite confidently that *she* gave it to me. How rude of me not to have remembered.

I love this gold and flowery thing, and I am delighted to be reunited with it.

T urnbull & Asser stand proudly as pretty much the defining idea of the British shirtmaker. But they build a splendid tie too. Jermyn Street, St. James's, is where Turnbull & Asser have long plied their trade. Their clientele could hardly be more distinguished: Pablo Picasso and Charlie Chaplin at the artistic end; Ronald Reagan, George Bush Sr., and Winston Churchill at the political. More glamorously, they have outfitted James Bond and the Kingsmen. You might have spotted the Prince of Wales's feathers on the label: Turnbull & Asser were the first outfitters to be awarded Prince Charles's Royal Warrant. All the clothing they sell is proudly marked "Made in England."

When passing Turnbull & Asser's I often pop in to reacquaint myself with an endearingly eccentric detail connected to their relationship with Churchill. In a glass case they display the siren suit in a comely shade of bottle-green velvet that they made for the great man. Winston himself invented the siren suit, a cross between an older-style boiler suit and a modern onesie. He loved their comfort and convenience and wore them not just at night, during air raids (hence the name, one supposes), but more and more in the daytime too as the war progressed. He was quite happy to meet Stalin and Roosevelt wearing them. The dozens of pictures of him in such creations even include a natty pin-striped number. They added to his appearance of a grown-up baby. In a romper suit, but with cigar in hand.

Lickable, likable candyfloss ties . . . a specialty of Duchamp. Despite the French name, the company originated in Suffolk, a county best known for having the good fortune to border Norfolk. Founded in 1989 by Mitchell Jacobs, an ex-buyer for the Mayfair boutique Browns, Duchamp is headquartered in Barnet. It has established a fine reputation for colorful men's clothing and accessories. I wore more Duchamp shirts and ties than any other make in my thirteen years hosting the BBC program *QI*.

The company was named after the French artist Marcel Duchamp because, according to Jacobs, "Duchamp turned everyday objects into art and I turned everyday icons of men's fashion into wearable art." Duchamp initially specialized in cuff links before branching into ties in 1992 and then clothing (shirts, trousers, blazers) in 2011. "There is a nod to chess, musical ideas and gentlemen's games throughout the product," proclaims the Duchamp website. Marcel Duchamp was indeed a keen (and very good) chess player as well as a painter and sculptor. There is, of course, so much else one could say about Duchamp and chess. Apparently, at one point during the war, Duchamp used to hand out regular chess beatings to Samuel Beckett—which would explain a lot . . .

have taken a Liberty. This tie turned up the other day in an old suitcase where it had no business to be hidden away. Arthur Liberty, like so many retailers and entrepreneurs in the field of the decorative arts in the nineteenth century, was hugely inspired by two major movements in art and design.

In the high Victorian era, Japanese culture became all the rage in Britain, inspiring Gilbert and Sullivan's operetta *The Mikado*, as well as a great deal of wallpaper, fabrics, and miscellaneous artifacts. As trade between Europe and Japan flourished, the arrival of woodblock prints by practitioners such as Hokusai, Kunisada, and Hiroshige had a transformative effect on the work of Western artists—Whistler, Degas, Toulouse-Lautrec, and, most notably perhaps, Vincent van Gogh were all avid collectors of Japanese prints.

The other great artistic energy of the time derived from John Ruskin, William Morris, and the Arts and Crafts movement, which morphed—with the help of continental European influences—into the flowing lines of Art Nouveau (detractors dismissed it as the "Noodle Style"). In the work of "decadent" artists like Aubrey Beardsley, the two influences came triumphantly together. And, you can say, in a more everyday manner they came together in the famous Liberty prints. The paisley print here has been another Liberty fabric staple since the 1880s.

LIBERTY
All Silk

After Hermès and Louis Vuitton, Lanvin stands as the third oldest of the great French fashion houses. Founded in 1889 by the formidable Jeanne Lanvin (1867–1946; she lived to see her beloved Paris liberated from Nazi occupation. It's always pleasing to spot when a great figure died knowing their side had won, isn't it? Poor Piet Mondrian expired in 1944. Did he leave the world thinking it was all over for his homeland, the Netherlands? Stephen, you're babbling, close the parenthesis and get on with it . . . Sorry, yes), who started as a Parisian hatmaker before moving on to designing haute couture apparel for women and their daughters. In the 1890s she located her business in the wildly prestigious Rue du Faubourg Saint-Honoré. Some of her finest work can be seen today at the Victoria & Albert Museum in London and New York's Met. Dresses of such grandeur have names: "Cyclone," "Jolibois" (Prettywood), "My Fair Lady," etc.*

Always pioneering, Mme Lanvin opened a sports department in 1923. Though let me stop you from thinking of JD or Sports Direct. No trackie bottoms and hoodies here: It was for the upper crust's tennis, swimming, riding, and skiing in Deauville, Biarritz, Monaco, and Saint Moritz. She really did hit pay dirt with Arpège, her legendary scent for women. As the 1920s roared on, she and her interior design colleague Armand-Albert Rateau began offering "furniture, rugs, curtains, stained glass, wallpaper, and more in the purest Art Deco style of the era," as the official Lanvin website puts it.

Menswear was added in the mid-1920s. I like to think of stylish Americans living the high life in Paris or on the Riviera, men like Cole Porter and F. Scott Fitzgerald, sporting Lanvin ties. There's always an understated elegance to their neckwear. This example, calm as it is compared to many of my other ties, is incandescently explosive set beside Lanvin's usual lines.

It's beautifully pimpled too, don't you think?

The company still flourishes today. There's a very fine shop on Mount Street in Mayfair—just round the corner from Berkeley Square, where nightingales sing.

* They do seem to have slightly lost the naming knack by the time they got to the 1980s: The Met's collection of Lanvin dresses has one from that era called the "Peasant."

Ah, jolly old Jermyn Street, and the very English name Charles Tyrwhitt. "Tyrwhitt . . . Tyrwhitt!" The call of a bird, perhaps? No, in fact it's pronounced "Tirrit." The older British families like to spring traps for the unwary: see also Mainwaring, Cholmondeley, Majoribanks, and Featherstonehaugh, pronounced "Mannering," "Chumley," "Marchbanks" and "Fanshawe," respectively. And let's not even start on Norfolk place names like Costessey and Happisburgh.

Charles Tyrwhitt, you might be forgiven for thinking, must be one of those venerable institutions like Turnbull & Asser or Hilditch & Key, founded when Queen Victoria sat securely on the throne, taxis were pulled by horses, and—in Alan Bennett's deathless phrase—"You could buy three pennyworth of chips and still have change from sixpence."

Actually the firm was founded, out of a Bristol student room, as recently as 1986 by one Nicholas Wheeler, who felt that he could make as good a shirt as anyone else.* His venture was a huge success. He and his wife, Chrissie Rucker, founder of the White Company, are reckoned to be worth close to half a billion of your puny Earth pounds between them. Lots of money in that white cotton, as James Caan nearly says in *The Godfather*.

Charles Tyrwhitt's core business remains the gentleman's shirt and accompanying necktie, no question. But, as the website says, "We've expanded from just shirts and ties to suits, shoes, casualwear, and accessories; we've opened thirty-eight stores worldwide; and grown from a single Bristol bedsit to now having 750 incredible people working for Charles Tyrwhitt around the world."

This tie here certainly grabs the eye, doesn't it? Bold and brassily confident, it can cheer a fellow up on a drab morning. That's the spyrwhitt.

* He does suggest, on his company website, that he named the company after his forebear "Sir Hercules Tyrwhitt, slain in 1067 on a bridge in Northumbria." Nicholas Wheeler's middle names are Charles Tyrwhitt. I wonder if he's also related to the nineteenth-century explorer and archaeologist Charles Francis Tyrwhitt-Drake?

What do we think of knitted ties? Well, I tell you a truth. When I was a youth, I was a great lover of all things James Bond, brutal, snobbish, sexist, and cruel as he could be. I thought, and still think, that Ian Fleming was a fine writer. Anthony Burgess and Kingsley Amis put me on to him at a time when all I had previously known was the cinematic Bond, fun as those films were. *The Spy Who Loved Me*, in particular (the book's story is completely unrelated to the subsequent movie), knocked me for six. I don't mind admitting, shallow and silly as it sounds, that I wanted to be Bond.

Fleming described 007 as favoring navy-blue sea-island cotton polo shirts with a knitted black tie. From Jermyn Street, of course. *Such* a Bond look. So naturally I did the same. New & Lingwood provided me with the correct Smedley's polo shirt and a dark-green knitted tie—they didn't have one in black. I would also go farther along the street to the legendary Geo. F. Trumper's, gentlemen's hairdressers, to buy Eucris aftershave, Fleming's (and therefore Bond's) preferred smell.

I decided that I liked knitted ties. The New & Lingwood is silk, as is the red Turnbull & Asser. They were made in Italy, unlike both companies' usual jacquard-weave silk ties, which bear the proud label "Made in England." Perhaps Italians know the secret of knitting silk. I finally alighted upon a black knitted tie in Brooks Brothers, on 44th and Madison, New York City, and I also found one there in my school's old-boys colors. Both are cotton.

Knitted ties have a softness and a lack of severe formality about them, which I like. Note how they get thinner where they fit into the shirt collar. They knot well too. But as for my coming close to Bond . . . well, it didn't take me long to realize, with a sigh of acceptance, that I was suited by nature to be a Blofeld, or perhaps a Goldfinger or a Drax—even a Miss Moneypenny or a Q. But never a Bond. Heigh-ho . . .

These are not just ties, these are M&S ties . . . M&S, Marks and Sparks—as British as *Blue Peter*, moaning, and HP Sauce. Starting as a "penny bazaar" in Kirkgate Market, Leeds, it was the first British retailer ever to post a profit of One Billion Pounds, Mr. Bond. To some, Marks & Spencer is a kind of thermometer permanently lodged up UK retail's fundament. When M&S is doing well, high-street Britain is a happy thoroughfare. When M&S falters, flounders, and fails—why, the kingdom totters too.

In the days of the St Michael label and the company's first forays into food, little old ladies around the country would drive their bankers and financial advisers crazy. "Let's look into more exciting stock. Maybe power generation?" "No thank you, dear. My Marks & Spencer shares have always done well enough for me, thank you." And for decades they proved those financial professionals wrong as M&S continued to outpace and outperform the competition. Two-thirds of all British women once wore M&S underwear. And in the 1980s . . . that chicken Kiev! Those dips, prawn mayonnaise sandwiches, and yum yums . . . "Not cheap," we would say of M&S produce and clothing, "but always such good value."

During the war, in France and Holland, new faces applying to join the Resistance would be tested—just to make sure they weren't German spies—by being asked questions about culturally defining institutions that only a true-born French or Dutch person could answer. Were that to happen here, we might ask newcomers into our resistance cells about Percy Pig and Colin the Caterpillar.

And its ties? All right, they aren't Jermyn Street or Milan in quality or artistry. But I've worn both of these without the slightest shame or embarrassment. Perfectly good throat-gear. I'll support M&S for as long as it's around . . .

This is going to stretch your tolerance of me to breaking point. It involves two elements that the world now finds unacceptable. Oxbridge. An all-male dining club. Eugh.

I went up to Queens' College, Cambridge, in 1978. The apostrophe does come after the "s"—it was founded by two queens. Yes, I know what you're thinking. Most amusing. The college had been a male institution since the 1440s. All that happily changed in my last year, by which time I was the president—or "Senior Member"—of the Queens' College Cherubs dining club. I don't want you to think of some braying Hooray Henry, pig-sticking, glass-breaking Bullingdon Club horror. We weren't Oxford, for goodness' sake. We had standards. But there's no denying it was what it was. A relic from an earlier time now, perhaps justly, held in deep contempt.

There was an initiation ceremony, which was more a test of the lining of one's stomach than anything else. When the wind changes, I can still taste that wild mixture of alcohols in my gullet, and I have to clutch at something to steady myself.

One of the features of the initiation was to tell the club what we would do to glorify the name of the Cherubs in later life. I said I would wear the tie on TV. I was very quickly as good as my word and wore it for appearances on *University Challenge*. That was nothing, though: A fellow initiate called Mike Foale promised he'd be a real cherub and fly to the heavens. We had no idea what he meant. But a few years later he joined NASA, served on Mir and the International Space Station, and still holds the record for the Briton longest in space (374 days).

Queens' College colors are dark green and white, hence the Cherubs tie's green stripe. Then there's blue for the heavens and cherub pink. My tie comes, like most official university and college merchandise, from Ryder & Amies, whose premises opposite King's College have been a feature of Cambridge life for more than 150 years. I know. Deeply disgraceful. I was young, feckless, carefree, and foolish. Now that I am old, feckless, careworn, and foolish I know better. Or do I . . . ? Feckful? Why the feck not.

Welcome, Ermenegildo Zegna (pronounced something like "Air-mennay-jeel-doe Dzainya"), a grand name in Italian fashion for over a century. In 1910 Ermenegildo and his brothers Edoardo and Mario took advantage of their father's woolen mill high in the Alpine foothills of Piedmont, in northern Italy, to produce high-quality fabrics to sell around the world. It was Ermenegildo's sons, Aldo and Angelo, who named the company after Papa and started, from the 1960s onward, to introduce suits, trousers, and finally a full range of shirts and accessories for men. To save time and spittle, most people refer to the company as "Zegna" these days.

With around five hundred stores and sixty-five hundred employees worldwide (pre-Covid-19, at any rate), and ten thousand plus merino sheep, Zegna is one of the foremost menswear companies in Italy—in the world, perhaps. Far be it from me to criticize the company's PR and marketing people, but their #whatmakesaman campaign is a little . . . well, perhaps a trifle . . . Tell you what, you judge.

> Masculinity is a state of mind, not a set of given rules. One thing does not make a man. Men have been learning that love is strength, kindness is power, openness is freedom. At Zegna men get undressed to be dressed, daring to bare their distinctive selves. Side by side with men for 110 years we continue to change, with them.

Well, I'm sure that after they had their brainstorming session they thought it meant something. Perhaps "men get undressed to be dressed" sounds better in Italian. "Daring to bare their distinctive selves" surely sounds deranged in any language.

But I mustn't be mean. After all, Zegna does create good things. This gorgeous greeny-gold tie . . . How I wish you could run it through your fingers. Feels like silk. Oh, it is silk. But somehow especially silky silk. Like an angel's inner thigh . . .

Stephen, go and have a lie down. You've done enough baring of your distinctive self for one day.

S imon Carter was quite the name in the 1980s and '90s. Especially known for original and quirky cuff links. The Aspirin design was hugely popular—little silver medicinal tablet shapes that unscrewed. The space inside could be used to stash . . . to stash whatever you had that could fit in there. Far be it from me to make a suggestion; your guess is as good as mine. Well, yes, you could keep that in there, I suppose—it's not for me to say. What made you think of such a thing?

He also designs watches, shoes, neckwear, and a range of menswear, from the casual to the well tailored. He won *Drapers* magazine's Menswear Brand of the Year in 2013. The flagship store is in Mayfair's Shepherd Market, with four others in the Greater London area. A sound and appealing British name, to be congratulated for staying independent and avoiding the temptation to expand too far and too fast, which so often ends in tears—ask any well-known chef or restaurateur.

Simon Carter trained as an immunologist, it seems, which we might think is a more useful profession these days than a fashioner—let's hope that, like a good gynecologist, he has managed to keep his hand in. Ho ho. No, but shush. Simon Carter, remember the name.

B ow ties, Stephen. *Really?* Well, not often. Just once in a while. Can't have more than a dozen, two dozen bow ties—tops. Not counting the black bow ties that one accrues over the years. A couple of the white for the very occasional need to don full formal tails. "The first two shallow shelves in the chest of drawers are completely filled with our white ties, sir," Jeeves tells Bertie Wooster. I can't claim such profusion. But, as I say, just occasionally I will go for a dicky bow. It can be hard not to look like a lazy television costume designer's idea of a Harley Street physician. Vets wear Clydella shirts and woolen ties; private doctors are always bow-tied. It's a TV rule.

Still. Maybe it's called a dicky bow because everybody who wears one looks like a dick. Heigh-ho.

THE FULL WINDSOR KNOT

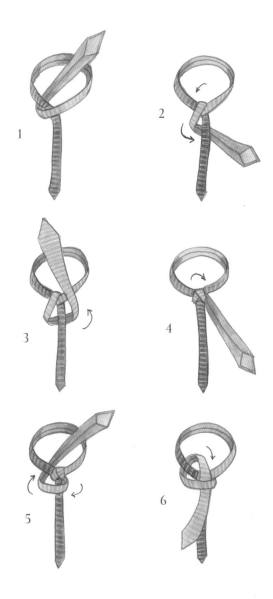

Silk! If there's a commodity in the world that's easy to take for granted it's the fine fiber produced by the larvae of the moth *Bombyx mori*. For five thousand years we've woven and wondered at it.

In the late 1600s more than ten thousand persecuted French Protestants (known as Huguenots) escaped to Britain, bringing with them their matchless silk-weaving skills. Despite James I's order that every English village should plant a mulberry tree (the silkworm larvae subsist on mulberry leaves), our climate had never allowed sericulture to thrive here. But thanks to the Huguenots the weaving thrived, or should that be *throve*? Local free-trade legislation and wage fixing caused Spitalfields, the hub of the trade in London's East End, to become unprofitable, so one original Huguenot family, the Vanners—who had begun weaving in 1740—moved from Spitalfields to Sudbury in Suffolk, via Basildon. They've been in Sudbury ever since, a blue-chip name in silk weaving. Amongst other fine silk goods, they produce superb seven-fold ties. (This name has nothing to do with the knot; it's how the highest-quality ties are made.)

Weaving has an interesting relationship to computing. The jacquard loom (invented in 1804) used a punched-card technology to allow the fast creation of complex and precise patterns. Essentially, it was programmable. The same punched-card principle lay behind the earliest computers, used by governmental tax departments, censuses, etc., right up until the development of the first digital machines in the 1950s. And it is digital computing that allows Vanners to combine modern technology and ancient craft in the creation of such a gorgeous object as this Liquorice Allsorts charmer. Vanners is not a household name, but it will always be venerated by those who value tradition, skill, and creative quality.

Your favorite? I like the pink coconut round ones myself . . .

L et me spin your melon, yank your chain, and tug your tether. This Fil à fil tie is a Fil à fil tie, but it is also not a *fil-à-fil* tie.

Stephen, this is wild and wanton raving. Have a sip of water, catch your breath, and start again. You're upsetting yourself. What can you mean? Out with it, man!

Well, *fil-à-fil* (with hyphens) is the French for "thread to thread," *fil* being the French word for "thread" or "wire," as in "filament." *Fil-à-fil* refers to a technique known in English as an "end-on-end" weave. In basic two-thread weaving, the crosswise or transverse yarn is called the "weft" (or occasionally the "woof"); the longitudinal, lengthwise yarn is the "warp." Warp and weft interweave to make woven cloth. In *fil-à-fil* the warp and weft alternate with dark and light threads (and sometimes threads of different thicknesses), creating what is known as a "heathered" effect. All the threads in one direction are one color, and all the crosswise ones are another color. It is most often used for cotton or linen cloth, or a silk/cotton mix, and is commonly found in Oxford shirts, for example. This Fil à fil tie is straightforward woven silk, with equal threading in warp and weft. Definitely not *fil-à-fil*.

Hermès (pronounced "Air-mezz") has nothing to do with the quicksilver messenger god of the Greeks. It was the family name of the founder, Thierry Hermès. As with Gucci, it all began with leather. For the first fifty years or so, Hermès made harnesses, bridles, and saddles (hence the carriage that you can see in their logo). Slowly, silk scarves, decorative homeware, watches, ties, and handbags were added. The Kelly and Birkin bags (named after actresses Grace and Jane) now cost upward of £10,000—ten times this for limited edition pieces. A Birkin bag once sold for $500,000. I know, mad.

Everything Hermès makes and sells is expensive, but at least they can claim that their products are all handmade by well-paid craftspeople in their legendary ateliers (studio workshops), usually one person per item. No sweatshop shenanigans with them. And they've managed to fight off the predatory moves of Bernard Arnault and his monster LVMH "luxury goods" behemoth. ("LVMH" stands for "Louis Vuitton, Moët, Hennessy," although it owns dozens and dozens more brands.) So there is that in their favor. There's something distressingly vile and self-conscious about many global high-price brands. That whole Singapore airport, Dubai mall vibe is frankly—I think—pretty trashy. Personally, I'd rather go about with a manky carrier bag than be seen dead with anything by Louis Vuitton. But for Hermès I do make a (doubtless absurd) exception. They dazzle.

W ho invented the shirt? What a strange question, you may think. It's like asking, "Who invented the kiss?"

Chemises of one kind or another have been worn since—and probably before—the ancient Greek male first shortened his chiton, or a daring Roman senator took a frustrated pair of scissors to his toga. In the case of the shirt, however, the august emporium T.M. Lewin of Jermyn Street (and countless other sub-branches—sixty-five in the United Kingdom alone) claim that their founder, Thomas Mayes Lewin, "created the first modern shirt with buttons down the front in 1898." They would argue, it seems, that men before 1898 didn't wear a "modern" shirt. And perhaps they are right.

Shirtiers (sadly there isn't such a word) nearly always make ties for the well-dressed beau too. To the storied (as Americans say) list of Hilditch & Key, New & Lingwood, and Turnbull & Asser, we can add T.M. Lewin. At one point they were the go-to shop for club, military, and old-school ties, but I think they've given up on that. Shirts remain their mainstay, but they offer handsome neckwear too. Like this dotty yellow lovely.

Gorgeously golden it may be, but what makes this specimen of neckjoy truly exceptional is the fact it is a "seven-fold tie." Common-or-garden ties are constructed from several pieces of patterned "shell," bulked out with cheaper lining and interlining, and machine-sewn. Seven-fold ties are made from a single piece of silk folded in on itself seven times—like an intricate paper airplane—and then hand-stitched. This requires at least twice as much silk, and is much more painstaking, but it produces the finest ties—the best to knot and to keep their shape.

The T.M. Lewin website, explaining the art of the seven-folder, proudly claims it to be "a true Jermyn

Street gentleman's style staple and something that takes real skill to produce." The Parisian shirtmaker Washington Tremlett is credited with stitching the first seven-folder in 1892, for an American customer. "Fast forward to the 1920s," T.M. Lewin proclaims, "and seven-fold ties were the preserve of well-heeled members of society." The art was all but lost, but then revived in the 1980s by the Californian tailor Robert Talbott. So this very British item was invented by a Frenchman for an American and brought back into fashion by another American. Often the way.

T.M. Lewin recommend the "four-in-hand" (page 228) as the best knot for a seven-fold. I think it looks fine indeed.

Tommy Nutter was a legend. As much a feature of the 1960s as David Bailey, Twiggy, and the Mini. Son of a café owner, he rose to "reinvent the Savile Row suit." In 1992 his life was sadly cut short at the age of forty-nine by AIDS. Amongst the great achievements of Nutter the Cutter was the dressing of three of the four Beatles on the *Abbey Road* cover. George opted out and plumped for denim.

One of Tommy Nutter's last creations was Jack Nicholson's purple suit for his role as the Joker in the 1989 Tim Burton *Batman*. Other clients included Mick Jagger, Elton John, even Stephen Fry, apparently (for a film role, though understandably Nutter tried to hush this up: Clothes hang on Fry like sacking on a hedge . . .). A whole generation of tailors and cutters were raised on Tommy Nutter's principles and methods.

'll ease you into this one gently, as people can be very disapproving. David Garrick (1717–79) would have heard his older relatives talking about the time of the Great Plague and Oliver Cromwell's ban on theaters. He and his friend and mentor Samuel Johnson (both from Lichfield) did much to raise the stage's reputation in the eighteenth century, and that of Shakespeare especially. Garrick became the first actor to shake off the profession's lowly "rogues and vagabonds" status. Painted by Gainsborough and Zoffany, he became the archetype of all great actor-managers. In 1831 a fine London club was founded and named in his honor.

This is the Garrick Club's famous "salmon and cucumber" club tie, perhaps the best known of all club ties. Mine is disgracefully clean. It is a mark of distinction for it to be egg-stained. Gull or quail ideally, or, at a pinch, duck—not plain old hen's egg. Nonsense like that aside, the club (now somewhat overrun by lawyers, politicians, publishers, and journalists) on Garrick Street, Covent Garden, still prospers. Largely thanks to A. A. Milne having bequeathed it a share of the rights to his *Winnie-the-Pooh* and other children's books.

I t's a classic tale. Benjamin Harvey, owner of a prosperous linen shop in London's modish Knightsbridge,* has a niece called Anne. Anne falls for and marries one of her uncle's employees—a Mr. James Nichols. When old Benjamin dies in 1850, his widow forms a partnership with Nichols and a new entity is born: Harvey Nichols.

There was a boy in my house at school called Dickson Poon. I wish I could say we were friends. He was in the year above me and probably looked down on me with (highly justifiable) contempt. We had no idea he would go on to become Sir Dickson, billionaire film producer, philanthropist, and owner of Harvey Nichols. His time of ownership has seen the store rise and rise in reputation, its name becoming synonymous with the aspirations of the Lady Di generation of Sloane Rangers, then of yuppies, and finally, of course, of the *Ab Fab* set, for whom Harvey Nicks became a shrine of pilgrimage.

It was final proof of the ascension of the city of Leeds into a new phase of post-industrial prosperity when the announcement was made that it was to have its own branch of Harvey Nichols. There are now stores in Manchester, Birmingham, Bristol, Edinburgh, and Dublin too.

But it is the Knightsbridge original, between Harrods to the west, Piccadilly to the east, and Chelsea and Belgravia to the south, that most draws the eye. Literally. The quality, originality, and daring of its window displays are unequaled in the capital. Dinosaurs, explosions, nudity, kinetic sculptures . . . over the years the arrangements have presented passersby and neck-craning bus and taxi passengers with alluring, appealing, and often avant-garde designs. The staff have had a reputation more for curtness than courtesy in the past. It can be bad luck—I've never met with rudeness there—but I accept my experience may not be typical.

This *is* a nice tie, though, with pretty rosettes hinting at the structure of an atom.

* Knightsbridge. Thirteen letters, three vowels. A Spanish friend told me it proved the impossibility of English.

Franco Moschino was a very playful designer. He started as an artist, drawing for Gianni Versace, and ended up founding his own label.

Moschino quickly established a reputation for innovation and larkiness: plug-socket drop earrings, quilted jackets festooned all over with bottle tops, a cashmere jacket with the words "Expensive Jacket" embroidered in gold on the back—that sort of thing. "Italy's Jean Paul Gaultier," some called him, but he was more gamesome and crafty, I think. He died in 1994, aged just forty-four; another life cut sadly short by AIDS. Here's to you, Franco Moschino, the joker in the pack.

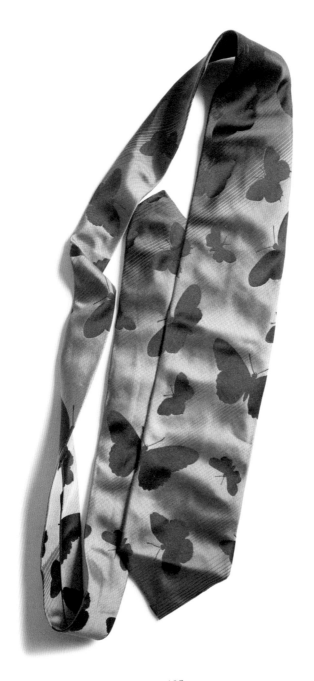

ermyn Street, London's Shirt Street, is home to many proud ampersands. Turnbull & Asser, New & Lingwood, Harvie & Hudson, Hawes & Curtis. But here is Hilditch & Key, inextricably linked to that splendid east–west thoroughfare to the south of and parallel with Piccadilly. Jermyn Street runs like a thread from a superior tweed through the history of English shirt-and-tie making, hat selling, hairdressing, and tobacco provisioning. For the last, Astley's, Davidoff's, and Dunhill's were the places to go for what were called "smokers' requisites." The smell of Dunhill's jars of Vanilla Cavendish pervaded the street when I was a soigné young arse-about-town. Bates the hatter. Taylor's and Geo. F. Trumper's the hairdressers. Fortnum & Mason (est. 1707). Wiltons restaurant (est. 1742). Such tradition.

Hilditch & Key were established in 1899. Charles F. Hilditch and W. Graham Key were already experienced in the Jermyn Street shirt business when they came together to set up their own businesses on Tottenham Court Road. Success soon followed them to SW1.

I'm a shameless hussy when it comes to shirt and tie buying. I'll pop into N&L one day, T&A, H&C, H&H, Tyrwhitt, Lewin, or Pink on other days (though Lewin and Pink both closed their physical shops during the pandemic, there are plans to reopen). As the mood strikes. No loyalty. But there are (or certainly were) old gentlemen who have always been Harvie & Hudson and would no more think of wearing a Turnbull & Asser shirt than they would a pair of Lycra shorts. "My grandfather wore Hilditch & Key and so do I." "We're a Hawes & Curtis family, always have been." That sort of thing. Maybe such types do still exist.

For now, let's hear it for the &mpersands.

This is perfect neckwear for those evenings where "black tie" may have been written on the invitation, yet you can be fairly certain that most men won't be dressing in full tuxedo and bow tie. A dark shirt and this glittery fellow can show respect for an evening without making one look like a waiter.

Liberty of London, still a proud name. The grand Tudor-revival flagship store (constructed from the timbers of HMS *Impregnable* and HMS *Hindustan*) squats athwart Great Marlborough, Carnaby, and Regent Streets, and squints at the London Palladium. Arts and Crafts and Art Nouveau are indelibly associated with Liberty—so much so that the Italian for "Art Nouveau" is *Stile Liberty*. The founder, Arthur Liberty of Chesham, Bucks, was, as you're no doubt aware from page 68, a great lover of Eastern styles: Their influence shows in the famous Liberty prints, which often feature miniature floral, paisley, and abstract patterns for furniture coverings, wallpaper, and, of course, scarves and ties.

When Joan Sims, as a French aristocrat in the *Carry On* film *Don't Lose Your Head*, hears about the slogan of the revolutionaries, she primly observes, "I don't care about the Equalities and the Fraternities, but I'm not having the Liberties." Well, quite . . .

The House of Etro is best known for its use of paisley. This example is something of an anomaly, but a rather stylish one.

Gerolamo "Gimmo" Etro founded his company in Milan in the late 1960s, but it is his four children who mostly run it now. Gimmo fell in love early on with Indian textiles and designs, and his use of paisley extended to more than just ties and scarves: Its distinctive swirl can be seen in Etro furnishing fabrics and its leather goods too. (The paisley pouches from the menswear section are the kind of accessory only a continental male could get away with, calling to mind that fine song "Gay or European" from the musical *Legally Blonde*.) On the Etro website there's a rather touching photo of a model trying to look comfortable while clutching his paisley manbag. Silly for us to be ill at ease with them when they're so useful.

Etro's son Kean once held a menswear show that included "cooked" shirts whose dyes were produced from blueberries, coffee, or salt and then baked in. Which is more or less how shirts of mine end up after a day's use, anyway. Like so many fashion brands, Etro has diversified greatly and is behind not just clothing but also footwear, handbags, jewelry, perfumes, textiles, and home furnishings. Unlike most Italian brands, however, Etro is not part of some huge luxury conglomerate, but remains in private hands. And pleasingly individual and quirky hands at that.

I remember when there was just one Paul Smith shop in all London. In Floral Street, Covent Garden. "Bliss was it in that dawn to be alive, But to be young was very heaven!" as William Wordsworth (250 years old in 2020) liked to say. So let the bells peal and hurrahs sound all around.

I insist you look, with firm insistence, very carefully at this tie. At its *shape*. It seems that this tie is trying to say something. Trying to sing something, perhaps. But what? If you can guess, you may award yourself ten points and the right to eat all the biscuits left in your place of residence.

All right, then. Well. A certain village in the West Midlands has been telling us about itself—its families, their lives, loves, interactions, and daily dramas—for more than seventy years. Some of us have such a fondness for this village and its happenings that we are proud to wear a tie that proclaims our affiliation, our devotion to that village and its inhabitants. Join in with me, all together now, "Dum di dum di dum di dum . . ."

"Barwick Green" is the theme tune of BBC Radio's *The Archers*, the world's longest-running drama. January 2021 marked the seventieth anniversary of the series beginning in earnest, on New Year's Day 1951, although five pilot episodes had been broadcast in May the year before. Thanks to that theme tune, every episode ends on a cliffhanger. "I think I will have that cup of tea after all . . ." Dum di dum di dum di dum! And you're hooked.

I joined Archers Addicts, the official fan club, back in the 1980s. I even compiled a crossword for their quarterly journal. If you are from anywhere else in the world other than the United Kingdom, the foregoing may mean little to you. I apologize. And there are Britons, I'm sorry to say, who do not listen to *The Archers*. I shan't use the word "traitor"—that's going too far. All the same . . . I mean to say . . . Dum di dum di dum di dum . . .

Older readers will remember how every high street and railway station used to boast a Tie Rack store. Some were little more than booths or kiosks. Along with Sock Shop, the chain exemplified a corner-turning moment in 1980s and '90s retail styles and habits. The first airport store opened in Glasgow airport in 1984, while the flagship store, at 295 Oxford Street, was opposite John Lewis. Much to my surprise, and I suspect to your surprise as well, dear reader, Tie Rack didn't die—it just went French. The brand now seems to be part of the Draeger conglomerate—along with Hallmark Cards. As well as still catering to one's neckwear needs, if one requires a very keenly priced scarlet Basque beret, then look no further.

The standard Tie Rack tie, with its standard Tie Rack label, is fine in its way. The label has a pleasing mauve sheen when you turn it in the light.

"A WELL-TIED TIE
IS THE FIRST SERIOUS
STEP IN LIFE."

Oscar Wilde

Beau Brummell, that superb arbiter of Regency style, was notorious for taking enormous care over the folding and tying of his cravats. Back then, there were different styles of knots that took some mastering. They had splendid names: the Mathematical, the Trône d'Amour (the "throne of love"), the Waterfall—that sort of thing. The story goes that a friend called on Brummell one morning for a cup of chocolate and a gossip. He found him in his dressing chamber, facing the mirror and carefully tying a knot. The floor was a white sea of dozens and dozens of discarded linen neckcloths. Brummell's valet caught the visitor's startled gaze and murmured, "Our failures, sir . . ." I can't remember if I read that story in the excellent Ian Kelly biography of Brummell, or if perhaps it popped up in the Stewart Granger biopic (Peter Ustinov played the Prince Regent). Whether it's true or not, it reveals the exquisite care the well-dressed Regency dandy would take in the folding and arrangement of his neckclothes. Lest you think of Brummell as some kind of foppish overdressed poltroon, dripping with enameled snuffboxes, quizzing glasses, and peacock colors, it should be noted that what he brought to style was a severe, but beautiful, simplicity. Black and white, the cleanest of lines. Not unlike the purity of the best Regency architecture. He made the mistake of insulting his erstwhile friend, the Regent, and died in penurious exile.

They say that the secret of succeeding in business for the long term is sticking to what you know. Your core market. You can certainly say that Hackett has now been around long enough to have shown that it understands this principle well. Few menswear retailers have established a more defining style and tone.

I thought when Hackett first appeared in the King's Road, Chelsea, in the early 1980s that they had made up their name as a kind of play on "hacking jacket," for that was the kind of clothing you could expect to find there. Tweed. Brick-red or lovat-green corduroy and moleskin trousers. Rugby shirts in the navy-blue school colors of a school that doesn't quite exist—the kind of rugby shirt that the buyer's girlfriend might borrow for herself to wear at the weekends. Guernsey sweaters. Green puffer jackets. Everything for the Sloane Ranger. In fact the name comes from founder Mr. Jeremy Hackett—nominative determinism at work, perhaps.

The venture caught on, and by the '90s there were Hackett branches all over town. Once the century turned I got to know them very well indeed. For a few years I was fitted out for the BAFTA Film Awards by Ozwald Boateng, before Hackett took over as the official maker. Eleven—or was it twelve?—times I hosted those ceremonies, and for at least six or seven of them I was Hacketted. The splendid Graham Simpkins was the gifted tailor given the irksome task of making suits for a man who could easily put on (or even, on rare occasions, lose) half a stone in a week. In P. G. Wodehouse's immortal phrase, it must have been like "a one-armed blind man in a dark room trying to shove a pound of melted butter into a wild cat's left ear with a red-hot needle." Well made, and as British as digestive biscuits, Hackett fills a niche perfectly—which is the definition of success in the natural world, and in the retail world too.

THE PRINCE ALBERT KNOT

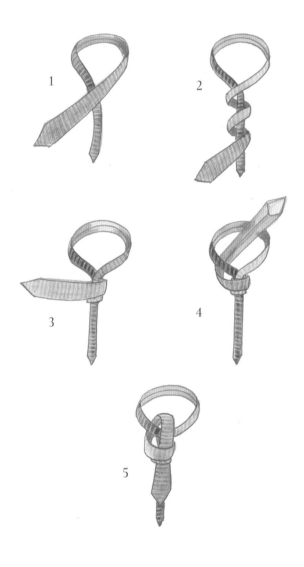

I will be seriously impressed if you can guess the genius behind this jazzy number. It looks like a 1950s creation, or maybe even something from an earlier hepcat, zoot suit age: the sort of tie that Cab Calloway might have worn when young. In fact it's the work of a hugely admired designer for men and women who debuted in his home country in the late '70s and worldwide the following decade. He acquired a name for exceptionally well-wrought avant-garde boldness and a look that was as dramatic as it was uncompromising. Strictly for the fashionistas back then. I could no more wear his clothes than I could dance for the Royal Ballet.

Our anonymous (for the time being) hero has designed for operas and movies, had an exhibition at the Victoria & Albert Museum dedicated to him, and has been enthusiastically collected and worn by such distinguished names as Elton John, Pina Bausch, Tina Turner, and the great conductor and pianist Daniel Barenboim. Mr. X's recent venture is an all-black watch for Hublot called the "Big Bang," though at well north of 20,000 poundlingtons it might better have been called "Big Bucks." All black is very much a signature look for this designer. So much so that he was a natural choice to design the New Zealand All Blacks' jerseys for the 2019 Rugby World Cup.

His name is . . . One more chance.

He is that Japanese master of line and form, the acknowledged poet of sharply tailored deconstruction—Yohji Yamamoto. His collaborations have been remarkable, with Adidas at one end and Hermès at the other. He even redesigned the classic Doc Martens boot. In the 2000s male and female models had worn the originals on his runway, so it seemed fitting for him to add his own flash of nonconformist style to that great British staple.

As for this addition to the #fryties collection . . . Well, it's a jazzy, snazzy dude that seems to demand untipped cigarettes and Brylcreemed hair: zoweee, tssssss, hot diggedy, pow!

This charming tie is from DÉCLIC, a company founded by Parisian Gilles Du Puy but headquartered in Australia. I bought this in Melbourne, where they have four stores. In French, *déclic* can mean the *click!* of love at first sight . . .

The Melbourne Cup is the horse race "that stops the nation"—bigger in Oz by far than our Derby or Grand National. The first Cup, run in 1861, was won by a horse called Archer. Hailed by *The Sydney Sporting Life* as an "honest and true a runner as ever was saddled," Archer had a distinct style—he ran with his tongue out. His winnings consisted of 710 sovereigns and a hand-beaten gold watch. Melbourne Cup Day— declared a public holiday in 1873—is a heck of an occasion. I've been a few times and had ridiculous fun.

I reckon that I bought this tie for my 2003 visit to the Flemington Racecourse. The course is shaped not unlike a pear, with races run in an anticlockwise direction. I must have hunted around the Melbourne shops and leapt with a *click!* when I spotted this jockey motif.

You may feel that ties like these ones are strange things. Thin as thin, which is sometimes a look one goes for. Slim ties were very popular back in the early 1980s, when we all turned our backs on the fat knots of the previous decade and went for a kind of '50s look combined with new mod, two-tone, and other post-punk styles that I didn't really understand. Could it possibly be that I was trying to look cool? A forlorn hope. I was never mistaken for the young Paul Weller, put it that way. But from time to time a pencil-thin tie is pleasing enough. And horizontal stripes make a good change too. You need the right shirt for the tie to work, I need hardly say.

You can't see the maker's name here; it's "Folkespeare." They are still around, so plenty of opportunities online to buy their ties, cummerbunds, cravats, and waistcoats. They are a subsidiary—or house brand—of Rael Brook, the shirtmaker whose advertisements in magazines were commonplace fifty years ago and whose very name summons a certain kind of menswear image. Not screamers, any of these ties, but all likable enough.

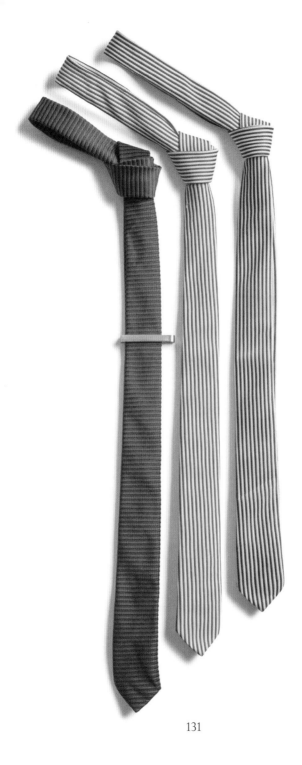

Doctors, surgeons, vets, and dentists all used to favor the bow tie. Unlike conventional neckties, they can't dangle down into a patient's face or open gizzard and guts. Those days are mostly past, though costume designers in TV dramas will usually pick them to denote an old-fashioned, often private, physician. Otherwise, bow ties are most associated in the public mind with Winston Churchill and—for my generation—the wonderful Frank Muir and formidable Robin Day. Who else wears them? It takes a bit of courage—easy to be dismissed as pompous, self-regarding, and, not to put too fine a point on it, something of a dick. So I tend to stroke mine fondly every now and again, but not much more than that.*

Of course, one use is as a substitute for plain black when a dinner jacket (or tuxedo, as Americans call them, after the exclusive village of Tuxedo Park in Upstate New York) is required. The dinner jacket was a Victorian invention, as is so much of modern dress. Lord Dupplin, as the story goes, who was a good friend of the Prince of Wales, had been invited on board the Royal Yacht. (Some versions of the story suggest Sandringham, but a yacht has a nicer ring, don't you think?) Unsure of the dress requirements, Lord Dupplin asked his tailor, Henry Poole of Savile Row, what to wear for the occasion. The resulting garment—an early version of the dinner jacket—was born. The Prince of Wales was quite taken with it, and by next season it was all the rage.

* You do not have permission to take the phrase "I tend to stroke mine fondly every now and again" out of context. Got it? Good.

Not a dazzling tie, this one, but it's just the kind of neckwear people would have owned eighty years ago or longer. Hope Brothers had seventeen branches in London, including Ludgate Hill, the Old Bailey, and a shop to the west in Bayswater, next to the Royal Oak pub on Porchester Road. There were also fifteen shops around the country—Norwich, Sheffield, Newcastle, Glasgow, and other "provincial" centers.

The firm was established in the middle of the Victorian era, its first shirt-making factory opening in the Cambridgeshire village of Littleport in 1882. The founder is given as one Thomas Peacock, who hailed from there. Shouldn't the company have been

called "Peacock's," then? Maybe that name would have suggested too much showiness for a straitlaced chain of British tailors. According to Littleport's local historians, Peacock set up the factory to provide work for local women during the great agricultural depression. Perhaps he chose the name for its symbolical value.

They offered military or "service" outfitting. One of the images on page 137 is an itemized invoice in elegant flowing handwriting for the kitting out of one Lieutenant Thoburn. The date is August 1915, the second year of the Great War. His "marching boots" cost 23/6 (£1.38½) and his spurs 5/3 (61½p). Two ties at 3 bob the pair, and a "whistle cord" for half a crown. To blow when leading his men over the top, I suppose. Fitted out for war at the cost of £25/17/0. That's £25.85, but worth £2,717.61 today (according to the Bank of England's marvelous CPI inflation calculator).

Hope Brothers were still equipping soldiers by the time of the Second World War, as well as advertising their school uniform line. For a period in the 1940s and '50s, they were also manufacturers of the England football kit. The Littleport factory was eventually taken over by Burberry. It is now a block of flats, although there is a commemorative plaque.

Hope Brothers, once a household name, now all but forgotten. You can almost smell the history coming off this tie.

Complete School Outfits

THE healthy Schoolboy has little respect for his clothes—*he* does not have to buy them —nevertheless, he likes to be as well turned-out as his chums.

Hope Brothers have carefully studied the requirements of the Schoolboy for nearly 40 years—both from his own and his parents' point of view—and so, specialise in good style Outfits made to give long service; and this for a very moderate outlay.

Furthermore, at each Juvenile Department we have authentic information regarding the actual requirements of all the principal Schools and Colleges in the country.

Here are a few prices of New Term Requisites:

Rugby Suits

Three garments in regulation School Greys, also in Browns. Well-cut from reliable, hard-wearing materials.
Prices for Boys of 10 years:
29/6   39/6   49/6

Trouser Suits

In serviceable School Greys and subdued shades of Brown.
Prices for Boys of 14 years:
35/6   41/6   45/6   53/6

> In all cases the prices quoted are for ages stated — other sizes proportionately priced.

Winter Overcoats

Of good warm Blanket Cloths, in a Selection of Greys and Browns.

Prices for Boys of 9 years:
21/6   26/6   32/6   41/6

Prices for Boys of 14 years:
27/6   37/6   45/6   52/6

Bring your boy to Hope Brothers for his complete School or College Outfit — for Shirts, Collars, Ties, Underwear, Hose, Footwear, Dressing Gowns, Trunks, Sports' Wear, and other School Requirements — or write for list of Complete School Outfits.

Hope Brothers

LTD.

Complete Outfitters
Chief School Outfit Establishments:

44 & 46, Ludgate Hill, E.C.4.
84-88, Regent Street, W.1.
129 - 133, Kensington High Street, W.8.
Branches throughout London and the Provinces.

The Royal Oak, Bayswater

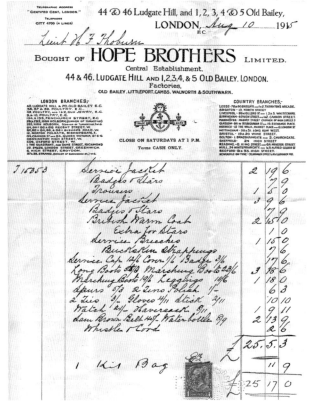

TELEGRAPHIC ADDRESS
"CENTIPED CENT, LONDON."
TELEPHONES
CITY 4700 (4 LINES)

44 & 46 Ludgate Hill, and 1, 2, 3, 4 & 5 Old Bailey,

LONDON, *Aug 10* 1915

E.C.

Lieut M F Thoburn

BOUGHT OF **HOPE BROTHERS** LIMITED.

Central Establishment.

44 & 46. LUDGATE HILL AND 1,2,3,4, & 5 OLD BAILEY. LONDON.

Factories.

OLD BAILEY, LITTLEPORT, CAMBS. WALWORTH & SOUTHWARK.

LONDON BRANCHES:-

COUNTRY BRANCHES:-

CLOSE ON SATURDAYS AT 1 P.M.

Terms CASH ONLY.

7 10653	Service Jacket		2	19	6
	Badges & Stars			7	9
	Trousers		1	5	0
	Service Jacket		3	9	6
	Badges & Stars			7	9
	British Warm Coat		2	15	0
	Extra for Stars			1	0
	Service Breeches		1	15	0
	Buckskin Strappings			7	6
	Service Cap 14/6 Cover 1/6 Badge 3/6			17	6
	Long Boots 48/0 Marching Boots 29/6		3	18	6
	Marching Boots 19/6 Leggings 19/6		1	18	0
	Spurs 5/3 2 Zino Polish 1/-			6	3
	2 Ties 3/- Gloves 4/11 Stick 3/11			10	10
	Watch 1/4/- Havresack 5/11		1	9	11
	Sam Brown Belt 45/- Water bottle 8/9		2	13	9
	Whistle & Cord			2	6
		£	25	5	3
	1 Kit Bag			11	9
		£	25	17	0

Good morning—or good mourning. Death is a subject that our culture avoids, certainly when compared with our ancestors. Even so, death will come for all of us.

Neckties are trivial things, by and large, but as a form of dress they play their part as units of meaning in the rhythms of our life. Mourning used to be as structured and ritualized as marriage, perhaps more so. Funereal black. Black mourning dress, black top hats trailing ribbons of black, black veils, black-edged writing paper, black armbands, black gloves, black jewels (jet), black crepe tied around the door knocker. There were established mourning periods (wildly exceeded by Queen Victoria after the death of her husband, Prince Albert). The actor Peter Cushing, a quite extraordinarily graceful, sweet, and modest man, wore black gloves for the rest of his life after the death of his beloved wife.

But we don't really know what to do. Religion offers its ceremonies, consolations, and, indeed, confident promises. There's a structure there, and wonderful language and music too. Most of us phone around our friends: "Shall I wear a black tie?" "Oh, she wouldn't have wanted that." We do our best, but our grief and sorrow are no longer displayed in our clothing and outward appearance. Perhaps that's good. There's no right or wrong answer here, I feel.

And so I have a black tie. The sight of it takes me back to funerals in churches, chapels, and crematoria, and reminds me of those I have known and loved who are now gone. Why it's Fortnum & Mason, more commonly associated with hampers and specialty teas, I can't imagine. But it's a tie more heavily freighted with meaning for me than any other I own.

F ounded more than two hundred years ago, Brooks Brothers can lay claim to being America's oldest men's clothing company: They made suits for Abraham Lincoln (including the one in which he was assassinated)—in fact, they have outfitted forty-one of the forty-six US presidents.

In the 1990s I bought an apartment on Madison and 77th Street. Madison Avenue had always been the first place I'd visit whenever I went to New York. On the corner of 44th Street (east of the famed

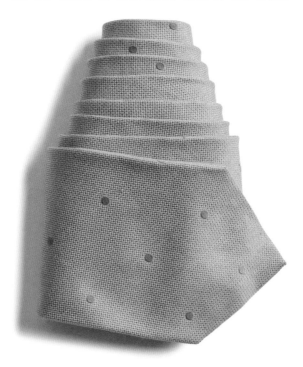

Algonquin Hotel) the flagship Brooks Brothers store, all dark wood and hushed splendor, was a magnet. Their "Golden Fleece" logo, a sheep hanging in a sling, derives from an old British woolmark. The name "Brooks Brothers" stands for a whole kind of America, a whole kind of style. The classic button-down Oxford cotton shirt (derived from the English polo shirt) defined the "preppy" look, which ex–Brooks Brothers employee Ralph Lauren took to a new level of high-street popularity. Elements of the style are now copied by many others, including more youthful lines; you can see the lineage in brands from Tommy Hilfiger and L.L. Bean to Abercrombie & Fitch.

In the late '80s Marks & Spencer bought Brooks Brothers. It's true! I remember for a while you could buy various M&S food items in the 44th Street store, while in the home Marks & Spencer branches, Brooks Brothers shirts went on display, largely to the bemusement of British shoppers. Crazy times. Sadly, in 2001 M&S sold the company on.

The neckwear Brooks Brothers is best known for is the "foulard" tie—a repeated block pattern on silk or silk/cotton (which has the advantage of allowing the knot to stay more snugly in place than with slippery silk). With a less shiny surface there's a faded, comfortable look that I rather like.

Brooks Brothers till I die . . .

I t's one of the most memorable scenes in a romantic comedy. The brown-and-white polka dots, the long expanse of green field, the divots . . . Vivian Ward, a.k.a. Julia Roberts, at the polo match in *Pretty Woman* feels, well, rather English. Is it any surprise that the Polo Ralph Lauren brand is meant to suggest an Albion aristocratic lifestyle?

Ralph Lauren set out to sell the American dream, and he used the aspirational appeal of preppy luxury to do it. In 1967, the twenty-eight-year-old Lauren convinced his boss to let him design a range of neckties from offcuts. He quickly added "Polo" ahead of his own name—he thought it sounded more English—and a sartorial lifestyle was born. Lauren's ties were different, wider and more colorful, and New York department stores snapped them up. Within twelve months, Lauren had sold half a million dollars' worth of neckwear.

In 1971 the brand's iconic logo of a polo player on his horse debuted, and just a year later, the classic Ralph Lauren polo shirt became a sensation. Its rainbow range in an initial twenty-four colors was as popular then as it is now.

The colorful rugby stripe of both these knitted ties appeals to me. Which is, I think, the sorcery of the Ralph Lauren marketing machine. In 1974 Lauren dressed the entire male cast of *The Great Gatsby*; remember Jay Gatsby's iconic pink suit? (Notice how often Ralph Lauren and iconic go together.) Polo Ralph Lauren became undeniably cool.

P aisley. The instantly recognizable Persian teardrop-at-a-slant design, known as a *buta* (meaning "shrub"), was an important symbol in Zoroastrianism, the religion of Zarathustra practiced by the ancient Persians and still by the Parsis of India today. We see it everywhere; indeed, in some of the most striking examples of computer-generated fractal imagery, especially the Mandelbrot series that seems to echo the recursive geometry of nature and the cosmos. Pleasingly, "Mandelbrot" means "almond bread" or "marzipan," so the attenuated almond shape of the paisley design seems rather appropriate for a fractal.

We call it "paisley," though in America it's some-times known as "Persian pickles" and the Welsh have been known to call the design "Welsh pears." It is the Scottish town of Paisley, however—a center of the textile trade in the nineteenth century—that has given it the most commonly used name. From there the paisley shawl and paisley pattern flooded the markets of the world. Paisley made the fortune of the Clark family, for one. Kenneth, Lord Clark, bought the grand nine-hundred-year-old Saltwood Castle in Kent, ran the National Gallery, and made the groundbreaking BBC documentary *Civilisation*. His son, Alan, was a phi-landering Conservative junior minister, famous for his brutally frank diaries and for being "economical with the *actualité*" (lying) back in the high days of Thatcher. All thanks to paisley.

The thread runs through much of our cultural history. It was hugely popular in the psychedelic '60s; something about its blend of intricate geometry and the organic flow of nature, its seeming to be part of the structure of everything, suited it to acid trips, light shows, and wild shirts and scarves. Suitable for a tie too.

This is the story of a whole human enterprise that—even in the age of the internet, cloud storage, universal archiving, and instant knowledge retrieval—has completely disappeared. All because of its name.

Once there was a retail menswear chain called Blazer. None of what follows would be true if they had called themselves Blennerhasset & Jones, or Popjoy & Co., or Wheedon & Weekes, or even Blaizer. But no, they called themselves Blazer, and so they have disappeared.

I liked Blazer. You might regard them as a sort of forerunner of Hackett. They sold slightly preppy menswear—not overwhelmingly Sloaney, as we used to say back in the 1980s, but with a definite air that mixed Fulham–Chelsea urban with Home Counties rural. They aimed their merchandise at a wider audience, however. The clothes were not too pricey, and their stores were in Covent Garden, not Knightsbridge or the King's Road. At least, that's how I remember it. As companies do, if they misplay their hands or if the cards don't fall right for them, Blazer disappeared. One day they were a feature of the high street, the next they had gone.

And because they called themselves Blazer, they are an absolute bastard to search for online. I typed in "Blazer stores," "Blazer Ltd," "Blazer and Co," "Blazer Covent Garden." Anything like that and you are returned hundreds of pages of links to shops online and off that sell . . . well, yes—blazers.*

What I can say is that they sold damned fine gear in their day, and I miss them. If only they'd been called Hipkiss & Welch or Winklefoam & Beadle, I might be able to source some choice items from eBay. Ah well—as the poet Whittier sighed, "Of all sad words of tongue or pen, The saddest are these: 'It might have been!'" Still, their cream-and-maroon dogtooth item in knitted silk wouldn't shame anyone's collar. Would go well in the summer months with . . . a blazer.

* I have since discovered that Blazer was bought by Moss Bros. in 1996, having been started by David Krantz—he of Racing Green, Space NK, and Planet Organic fame—in the early '80s. *Plus ça change* . . .

Canali is one of those stores you pass by in high-end malls for years without thinking of popping in. Another Italian fashion house at the "luxury" end of the market. I can't pretend to know *much* about them—I think this tie is the only thing by them I've ever owned. And as you can tell by the fact that the tag is still attached to it, I've never even worn it. A shame, as it's rather a princely tie with its play of colors, sheen, and texture.

The company was founded in 1934 (don't mention Il Duce) by Giacomo and Giovanni Canali and it stayed in the family until 2007. It produces exclusively menswear items, manufacturing clothing, shoes, and accessories, and offers a *su misura* service for made-to-measure trousers, blazers, suits, and shirts. It claims to have 180 "boutiques" around the world and to employ 1,600 people, mostly in its seven factories in Italy.

Like many such companies it has, over the decades, supplied film actors with clothes for select productions; in recent years, most noticeably George Clooney in the excellent *Michael Clayton*. If ever a man can show a suit in its best light, it has to be the Cloonster. Do you remember the overcoat he wore in that film? Just perfection.

For what it's worth, "Canali" means "canals" in Italian. Somehow it just wouldn't work as an English surname, would it? Except possibly as some sort of strange mobster nickname. "Say hello to Joey Canals . . ."

149

Was "Primavera" (the Italian for "spring") an in-house design studio for Tie Rack? Did the extra word on this tie's label indicate a "designer tie," with a corresponding hike in price? The word "designer" was beginning to be peppered onto everything from sunglasses to boxer shorts in the retailing heyday of the 1980s. Can we discern a distinct difference here from *other* Tie Rack morsels? This fine specimen is 100 percent silk and made in Italy, and has an almost watercolor effect, perhaps. It does seem to be far more free-spirited and arty than most other Tie Rack ties.

It's of no great matter—doubtless some marketing figure decided there should be this variation in labeling. Such is often the way of sartorial splendor. Tie Rack has—at least on the British high street—gone to retail heaven, where it is kitting out the angels in good, but not great; fine, but not fabulous; quality, but not costly, neckwear. I wish them a blissful eternity, or as Horatio almost phrased it to the dying Hamlet, "Good night, sweet Tie Rack, and flights of angels sing thee to thy rest!"

I am not completely confident about the source of this tie. It's labeled "Searle," and the tie itself has a mod feel, or perhaps a pleasing lick of '50s jazz about it. There were Searle stores in Manhattan that sold clothing for men and women—a specialty, apparently, was shearling coats for ladies. But I believe they went out of business more than ten years ago. Maybe the tie was one of theirs. I like it enough to want to know, at least.

Of course, it's not *such* a big deal (or "not that big of a deal," as Americans say*) not to know the origin of a tie, but there is no doubt that there's some satisfaction to be derived from knowing the time and place of purchase. Like Proust's madeleine, a tie can release floods of memory. If, for example, I did buy the Searle in Manhattan some time before 2009, then I can consider where and what I was doing, how contented or blue I might have been, whether or not it was bought for some kind of event. Back then, if I was invited to publication launches, Broadway first nights, or private views of an artist's show, I always wore a tie. And sometimes, if I hadn't time to get home before whatever it was started, I would stop off at a store on my way to the event in order to buy one. I'll probably never know . . .

* Whenever I write that something is said in the United States, a peeved American will comment that *they* have never used such a phrase in their life. I'm damned, though, if I have received a single email from an American in the past five years that doesn't include some kind of reaching out. "I'm reaching out to ask if . . . ," "I have been asked to reach out to all people who . . . ," etc. There's nothing especially wrong with the phrase, and it is gaining "traction" here, but . . . *Stop it, Stephen.*

153

Would you be surprised to learn that this shining example of a tie represents the Hawks' Club? And that the Hawks' Club is a Cambridge invitation-only club for sportsmen? (Yes, I'm afraid it is still wholly male, since its founding in 1872.)

The Hawks' Club "represents the best sportsmen at the University of Cambridge." The election process recalls that of a London club: Prospective members must be "proposed" by an existing member, then seconded, and finally have their application signed by six more current members. Unlike Whites, say, or the Garrick, the proposer is normally the team captain for the relevant sport, nominating someone who has represented Cambridge against Oxford in a Varsity match.

Ah, the Varsity match. You are perhaps aware that in Oxford and Cambridge there are such things as sporting "Blues." You can represent Cambridge, whose color is light blue, on the hockey field, for example, for just about every game of the season and be far and away the best player on the pitch for all of them, but if you miss the Varsity game, the one match against the dark blues, Oxford, you will not be awarded your Blue. A Blue, for either side, means you play against the Enemy.

issoni, the maker of these two wonderfully bold ties, is one of Italy's most recognizable fashion houses. Particularly for a colorful zigzag pattern that I've never quite fallen in love with. Missoni's founders, Rosita Jelmini and Tai Missoni, met at the 1948 Olympics in London. Tai had been making knit tracksuits with a teammate in Trieste. In the 1950s, Rosita and Tai—now married—started producing handmade knitwear in the small Italian town of Gallarate. It became *the* clothing of choice for fashionable locals, and by 1958 the brand had become so successful that they showed a collection in Milan. The business was originally called Maglificio Jolly (Joker Knitwear), but when an order for five hundred dresses came in from the Italian fashion capital, Missoni was born.

Missoni tapped into the 1960s mod style—sharp tailoring, knitted polos, desert boots—as well as the burgeoning sexual revolution. The Missoni look was bright, slinky, and often scandalously sheer. When *Vogue*'s iconic editor in chief, Diana Vreeland, gave the brand the *Vogue* stamp of approval, Missoni quickly became a household name in America. Today it's still a family-run business, with their factory located near the town of Sumirago, close to the Italian Alps.

THE PRATT-SHELBY KNOT

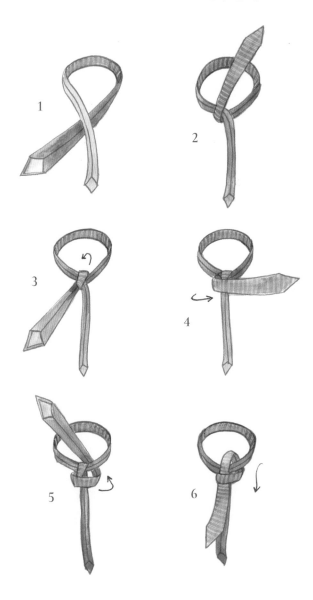

Ruth Strauss died of an incurable lung cancer that affects nonsmokers in December 2018. Her husband, the former England cricket captain Sir Andrew Strauss, set up the wondrous Ruth Strauss Foundation to raise awareness of nonsmoking lung cancers and to offer professional emotional support to families facing the death of a parent. Ruth was only forty-six years old and left behind two children, then aged ten and thirteen.

In 2020 I attempted to use a cricket bat to hit a ball up in the air twenty-six times in a row. It was a demonstration of extraordinary physical skill, I assure you. The bat, signed by members of the England team, was auctioned, and raised a very happy amount for this very worthwhile charity.

alvin Klein. There's a name to conjure with. It is more or less agreed that Calvin Klein invented the whole designer label Thing. Or did he? Maybe it was Jeffrey Banks—an American designer who mustn't be confused with our Jeff Banks, the British fashion designer and presenter of the BBC's *The Clothes Show* throughout the 1990s. The story goes that Jeffrey Banks, who worked for Calvin Klein at the time, once sent him a brown T-shirt on which Klein's name had been silk-screened. It was meant as a one-off present, a cute gift. Klein's business partner, Barry Schwartz, received it and assumed it was the prototype for the new design of tee. It went into production—the rest is history.

Soon Calvin Klein's astoundingly successful line of jeans, with his name prominently displayed on the rear pocket, exploded into the world. Underwear was previously something men rarely thought of— the accepted retail wisdom was that women bought three-packs of white undies for their sons, husbands, or boyfriends. But all that changed with the aggressive marketing campaigns for Calvin Klein underwear, most memorably the ads featuring a young white rapper called Marky Mark, now known to us as Mark Wahlberg. Fragrances such as Obsession and Eternity were enormous successes too, propelled by similarly powerful TV and billboard advertising and the use of big-name models.

The designer label craze was born. It quickly became impossible to buy any piece of clothing, no matter how humble, that didn't prominently carry the maker's name or logo as a ... well, a badge of something. I can just remember a time when they didn't do this. But clothing almost looks naked without it now.

Calvin Klein ruled the 1980s and '90s with a kind of minimalism, not often very colorful, but always cleanly designed. He is not really known for ties, and this one is not overwhelmingly exciting. But 80 percent silk, 20 percent cotton makes for a soft feel. And it is the only Calvin Klein I own ...

You'll be entirely forgiven if the name "Prochownick" is new to you, and I will offer even larger helpings of clemency and absolution if you confess to being surprised to learn that the name belonged to a distinguished Italian design house, centered for 140 years in Italy's fashion capital, Milan.

In 1880, Hermann Prochownick arrived in Milan from his native Leipzig and began producing ties, scarves, and foulard squares in silk and wool. According to the wonderful *Mam-e Fashion Encyclopedia*, "In the 1930s, his sons Carlo and Luigi Italianized their surname to become Procovio* (but they kept the original company name). They expanded the business and started exporting abroad." The factory was based in Via Bandello in Milan, though sadly it is now closed.

In my opinion this Prochownick tie is well juicy and cowing lush. I am pretty sure, but wouldn't bet on it, that I bought it in the United States. Prochownick ties are easy enough to get hold of still, and I think the name should be better known. It's quite possible, of course, that my assumption that you are likely to be unaware of the name is merely a reflection of my own brazen ignorance. You may well have been talking about Prochownick and little else for years. Possible, but unlikely . . . ?

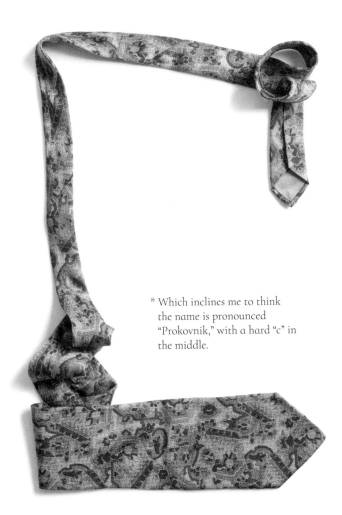

* Which inclines me to think
the name is pronounced
"Prokovnik," with a hard "c" in
the middle.

A mystery, my friends! This tie has me completely stumped. I cannot remember where or when I bought it; I know only that I think it rather fine and probably of late 1980s or early '90s vintage. Is "Davies" a label that briefly belonged to George Davies, the serial brand-entrepreneur who gave the world Next, George at Asda, and Per Una (which he sold to Marks & Spencer for £125 million—all part of his and M&S boss Stuart Rose's cunning way of repulsing the hostile takeover attempt of Philip Green)? An extraordinary man, George Davies, but I'm damned if I can find any evidence that there was an actual "Davies" connected to him. There is a Euphemia Sydney-Davies, the name of a former Alexander McQueen trainee. But this isn't her work, I think. There is the great and grand Davies & Son of Savile Row, established 1803. "In over two centuries of bespoke tailoring we have made garments for four Kings, seven Crown Princes, two US Presidents and innumerable Knights of the Realm." I'm pretty sure they didn't make this offering for plain old, common old Mr. Fry, however.

A ha. A "Chevalier" tie. A Tie Rack spin-off, which looks to be greatly influenced by Versace. The label is adorned with tricolors—was this lovely specimen the "French" equivalent of Tie Rack's (Italian) "Primavera" line?

The design seems lifted from a Renaissance woodcut of some royal or imperial procession. If the flags on the trumpets had been blazoned with double-headed eagles, the procession would involve a Holy Roman Emperor. And there is, of course, a very famous woodcut (and very large: It stretches across more than 130 pages, or almost 180 feet) depicting "The Triumphal Procession of Maximilian I" (1516–18) by Hans Burgkmair and others. It seems to me that this tie, with all its pomp and glory, is certainly inspired by such things.

Dame Vivienne Westwood is a legend. Once a primary school teacher, she helped bring punk and avant-garde fashion into the mainstream. Her first shop, set up in 1971 with Malcolm McLaren, was located on 430 King's Road in Chelsea. They designed fetish wear and sold it to prostitutes. Her band tees, co-designed with the Sex Pistols a few years later, remain prized: cut-up Union Jacks and Queen Elizabeth II with a safety pin through her lip. But it was her "New Romantics" sensibility from the '80s onwards—design drawing on historical silhouettes—that made Westwood famous. Military uniforms, the Tudor court, belle époque corsetry, and the British royal family all provided inspiration.

Is there something subtly punkish about both these Westwood ties? They're certainly eye-catching. A note, too, about the Westwood orb. In the mid-'80s, Vivienne set about designing a knitted jumper that Prince Charles might wear. A coat of arms, griffons, the thistle for Scotland, the leek for Wales, the shamrock for Ireland, the crown and orb from the crown jewels—all would be present. To make the whole thing feel modern, Vivienne added a ring around the orb, like the satellite ring around Saturn. This eye-catching logo has been in use ever since.

This wonderful tie is in the manner of Fornasetti. I did once come across an umbrella stand with the same motif.

Piero Fornasetti, born in Milan in 1913, was a creative force of nature. A designer, painter, engraver, and interior designer, he was more interested in the surface of something than its shape, covering everything from furniture and textiles to tableware in surreal, hand-painted images. He is said to have created more than eleven thousand items in his lifetime.

Fornasetti credited many influences. He was inspired by Greek and Roman architecture and neo-classical facades, though it was the face of Lina Cavalieri—an opera singer once considered the most beautiful woman in the world—who served as his muse. Versions of her face continue to be printed on everyday objects by the company today—chairs, matchboxes, cushions, and collectable plates—as part of the *Tema e ariazioni* series. Fornasetti wastepaper bins retail for as much as £1,000, while larger pieces of furniture can be bought secondhand for £20,000.

Once you've seen a few examples, it becomes easy to spot a Fornasetti motif. Monkeys, architecture, the sun and moon, hot-air balloons, butterflies, and fish—all are part of a Fornasetti world that plays as much with imagination as it does with reality. It's a style often imitated, though no one else has ever quite captured the wit and playfulness of a Fornasetti original. Though I am fond of this admirable attempt.

"BEING PERFECTLY WELL-DRESSED GIVES ONE A TRANQUILITY THAT NO RELIGION CAN BESTOW."

Ralph Waldo Emerson

THE VAN WIJK KNOT

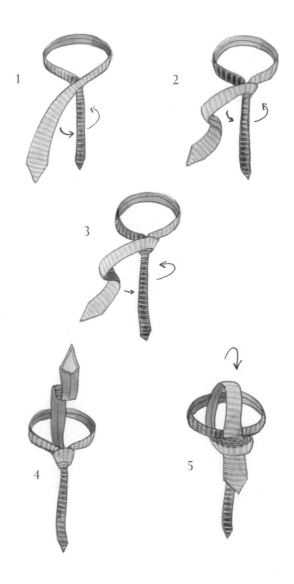

N eal & Palmer are another bespoke menswear outfitter, though they were established a bit later than many of their neighbors, in 1993. Unlike their Jermyn Street colleagues, there isn't a long and illustrious history of famous customers—yet, at least. I have seen a picture of Rod Stewart in their shop. According to their website, the "Neal and Palmer label means the finest of British bespoke menswear. . . The use of hand-embroidered fabrics, velvets, linens, fine wools, silk and brocades, give the individual man the look they want with the knowledge that they are wearing the best available." Neal & Palmer do a brisk trade in morning suits and black tie, amongst other things. They have a fantastic coat of arms particular to them, with a Neal & Palmer waistcoat flanked by a lion rampant and a horse. In place of the chain is a measuring tape.

The N&P tie here is certainly luxe in feel and appearance. It's made of a heavy raw silk and is wider than is typical. I can't recall ever having worn it, though it would look very smart with a morning suit, should the occasion present itself.

When I was young, so much younger than today, I lived in Draycott Place in Chelsea, just off the King's Road. I became enamored of the Reiss store there and especially its wonderful jumpers. I still have most of them. It frightened me how much they cost. I had just left university and was starting out, but even though I couldn't afford it I just wasn't able to stop myself splurging on things Reiss.

The company was founded by David Reiss in Bishopsgate, not far from Liverpool Street Station, in 1971, and produced exclusively menswear, mostly suits. While on the subject of the garment business, I love the words "suitings," "trouserings," and "shirtings," which refer, I think, not to the items themselves, but to the fabrics used to make them up. No one says "pantings" or "vestings," so far as I know, which is a shame—but there we are. Anyway, Reiss added womenswear and grew and grew, and it has done especially well lately. You see outlets in airports and shopping centers everywhere these days; they've even got a branch in Greenwich Village, New York, apparently. They are justly proud of their 2019 designs being showcased on "the largest digital screen in Europe" in Piccadilly Circus.

The older of these two Reiss ties, the cheerful yellow one sparsely dotted with comely little flowers, hasn't been well kept, for which I apologize. Yellow is perhaps my favorite color, all in all, though I have been surprised by how the great majority of the ties I own seem to be red or mixtures of red. But a Reiss tie will always make me think of Chelsea punks in mohicans, the Queen's Head in Tryon Street (a warm and friendly little gay pub), and those glorious Sloane Rangers in the heady days of Lady Di, Dire Straits, and the Rubik's Cube.

181

The use by adults of images associated with children is now so common as to be unworthy of notice. Yet, once upon a time, things were very different. As Saint Paul remarked, "When I was a child I spake as a child, I understood as a child, I thought as a child; but when I became a man, I put away childish things."

When I was growing up, an adult wearing school sports items like training shoes, tracksuits, and baseball players' caps; eating pappy foods; drinking sugared fizzy drinks; playing electronic games; and watching films about super-beings who can fly or zap out lightning or silk filament from their fingers—well, the idea was unthinkable. Any grown man who dressed, ate, and behaved like that would have been looked on as unwell. It's not for me to talk here about the infantilism of the Western male (and it is mostly males, I think)—goodness knows I'm as much a part of that culture as anyone else—but the fact is that, when I grew up, Disney was for children. There were no videos or other ways of seeing Disney products except in the cinema or on Saturday morning TV shows. A Mickey Mouse wristwatch had an ironic cachet, perhaps, but that was about it.

But in the late 1980s all that changed. Disney Stores appeared in high streets and shopping centers, and they didn't seem to be just for children now. This coincided with the worldwide rise of the Big Mac, and Hollywood turning out blockbusters like *Star Wars* that would never have been considered suitable for grown-ups twenty years earlier.*

As this tie so aptly demonstrates, there's nothing wrong with a bit of silliness. Ties can easily be pompous and stuffy. Sometimes a childish and frivolous one is a useful way of showing that you don't take yourself too seriously. Though it can make you look like a bit of a ho-ho wag, the wacky uncle who always tells jokes and possibly even owns clockwork yackety-yak false teeth and whoopee cushions . . . *shudder*.

* Before you write in, I know the first *Star Wars* film was released in 1977.

L uise Steiner is an Austrian family-run company that specializes in colorful costume accessories. They often lean into the "Rosegger" trend of traditional national clothing. Peter Rosegger, the trend's namesake, was an Austrian writer and poet known for his novels describing provincial life.

The tradition of combining red and green is an old one. For the ancient Celts, holly plants, with their evergreen coloring, were there to keep Earth beautiful in the dead of winter. During the fourteenth century, red and green were frequently paired on painted medieval rood screens. But the modern association of these two colors with Christmas is thanks to one individual: Haddon Sundblom.

Haddon Sundblom, an American artist of Swedish descent, was hired by Coca-Cola to draw a Santa Claus for the company's ads in 1931. Before Sundblom, Victorian Christmas cards frequently showed a Santa adorned in green, red, or even blue robes. The Coca-Cola Santa was an instant hit, and Sundblom spent the next thirty years illustrating Father Christmas. To this day, his version remains, arguably, the most recognizable Santa in the world.

This *isn't* a Christmas tie. And yet, I always think of Alpine landscapes, Kris Kringle, and roaring fires when I wear it.

Dainty green tree frog. Crucifix toad. Dahoping sucker frog. At last, a piece of sartorial wonderment as educational as it is beautiful.

For many cultures, the humble frog has been a symbol of fertility, regeneration, and rebirth. After the annual flooding of the Nile, frogs were born in vast numbers, and they came to be associated with the fecundity the yearly event brought to the area's arid lands.

The Egyptian goddess of midwifery, Heqet, was frequently depicted as a female with the head of a frog, and Egyptian women would wear jewelry in her image to court her favor. The Aztecs saw the toad as embodying the eternal cycle of death and rebirth, represented as Tlaltecuhtli, the Earth Mother goddess.

For the Greeks, the frog took on a degree of licentiousness, associated as it was with Aphrodite, the goddess of love and beauty. In Irish folklore, frogs were seen as creatures of the underworld and linked with witchcraft—hence their frequent appearance in the preparation of potions and spells. If a child developed whooping cough, putting a frog into their mouth three times and letting it swim off in water would cure the affliction. Students at Hogwarts, of course, consider chocolate frogs a popular wizarding treat.

However one feels about frogs, I am happy to report that there are a fair few similar neckties, all made by the Museum Artifacts brand, on eBay. Happy gigging.

In 2018 I spent a glorious few months in Niagara-on-the-Lake, Ontario, performing my Mythos Trilogy for the Shaw Festival. It was a happy time, and in the way that certain items do, this particular tie takes me right back to that summer.

I am hugely fond of its strong colors and shapes. The tie was purchased from Oscardo, a Toronto store that curates a wonderful selection of Canadian and Native art gifts. The company, which started in 1987, was originally focused on neckwear after its founders, the Lulka brothers, acquired an existing tie maker. They now

supply everyone from museums and private galleries to Canada's National Parks stores.

This particular tie was designed by Chipewyan Dene artist John Rombough. Of it, John says, "On an early spring morning, the bear in his elements is walking alongside grandfather rocks. As the Ancestors watch over the land, the Ravens welcome the bear from a long winter's nap."

Glorious, indeed.

ricket is a deep and abiding love. Those who follow the game will know about "benefit years," when matches are played and dinners held to boost the incomes of long-serving players. I've been to many such dinners, spoken at some, and supported others as best I could. Buying a Derek Pringle tie in 1992 was the least I could do in recognition of a fine servant of Essex and England. An all-rounder perhaps better remembered for his bowling ("Pring the Swing," we called him) than his batting, Pringle was a highly intelligent and likable presence on the field of play for ten years. He is now a well-respected cricket writer. Note the three notched seaxes (wide, curved swords) alternating with three lions, indicating Essex and England.

191

T he maker of the tie pictured here, Dehavilland, turns out to have been the own-label tailoring line of that now defunct menswear chain Blazer, whose sad disappearance from the high street and the internet I covered on pages 146–147. Founded by David Krantz in 1979, Blazer—and thus Dehavilland—were subsequently bought for £5 million by Terence Conran's retail conglomerate Storehouse (Mothercare, Habitat, BHS, etc.), which in turn sold the company on to Moss Bros. in 1996. Coincidentally, that same year Mr. Krantz sold his next venture, the upmarket casual-clothing group Racing Green, for £19 million to Burton.

Moss Bros. and Burton were the two best-known names in twentieth-century British high-street menswear. Demob suits, special-occasion hire, smart outfits for men who didn't often wear a suit or think too much about clothes. Both companies struggled to stay afloat in the retail waters of the 1980s and '90s. Fashion, foible, and fickle fancy make profitability, and even solvency, a game of Buckaroo in the clothing business. You can be forced by shareholder pressure to pay for the services of some dickbrain of a "brand consultant" or "PR guru," who'll have you spend gazillions on redesigning and "reinventing" your shops, and radically changing your lines, logos, and layout. The result? You alienate your loyal customers and cause snorts of derision from the young, who can see with piercing clarity that you are trying to appeal to them. And nothing will cause them to stay away more completely than that. A painful experience suffered by many a company. And this was before the explosion in online retail.

Burton ended up having the happy privilege of belonging to "Sir" Philip Green of the Arcadia Group. Gone for a Burton, indeed. But one doesn't wish them ill. It's tough out there. Nor the Brothers Moss, who have dressed men so well for 170 years. They at least have managed (as far as I can tell) to stay independent.

David Krantz is, I hope, enjoying his money. Thanks for the tie, Mr. Krantz.

THE KELVIN KNOT

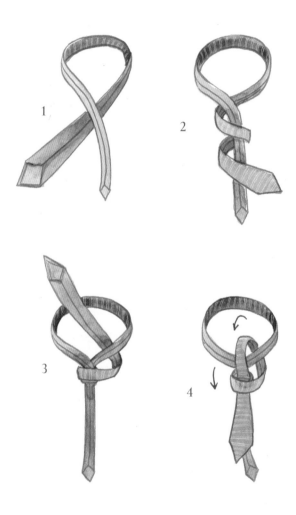

I n 2010, the delightful students, scholars, and persons of Cardiff University awarded me the distinct privilege of becoming an Honorary Fellow. A year later, I became patron of the university's superb Neuroscience and Mental Health Research Institute.

Cardiff University, originally University College of South Wales and Monmouthshire, began in 1883, with the formal Royal Charter dated to 1884. Pupils could study biology, chemistry, English, French, German, Greek, history, Latin, mathematics and astronomy, music, Welsh, logic and philosophy, and physics. The college carries the distinction of being the first in Wales to allow women to enroll, though until 1893 the college was not allowed to award degrees, since it wasn't an independent university. Instead, students would sit examinations for the University of London or go on to further study elsewhere, often at Oxford or Cambridge. A little convoluted, one could say.

While my Welsh language skills are very poor indeed, I am incredibly proud to be an ambassador for both the university and the institute. I shall continue to wear this tie and exclaim "*Gwirionedd, Undod a Chytgord*" (or "Truth, Unity and Concord"—the university's motto), on appropriate occasions.

Shep and Ian Murray founded Vineyard Vines in 1998, after quitting their Manhattan desk jobs to chase the American dream. As Shep and Ian put it, "they started selling ties so they didn't have to wear them."

The Murray brothers grew up spending their summers on the preppy enclave Martha's Vineyard, an island just off the southeastern coast of Massachusetts in the United States. Cape Cod, Martha's Vineyard, the Kennedys, Harvard University, Boston . . . there is a sophisticated patina, a ritzy finish to the state. Massachusetts has its blue-collar Irish, its rural poor, but the image is still that of patrician wealth and founding history. Much of the prosperity of nine-teenth-century Massachusetts derived from the now disgraced industry of whaling. The center of this grisly trade was the island town of Nantucket, which, like Martha's Vineyard, is now a neat and pretty, if somewhat sterile, heritage and holiday resort. It is a pompous and priggish error to judge our ancestors according to our own particular and temporary moral codes, but nonetheless it is hard to understand how once we slaughtered so many whales with so little compunction.

The company logo for Vineyard Vines is a jolly-looking pink whale, a somewhat incongruent nod to the island's heritage. Reasonably priced, with jaunty patterns and good-quality silk, a Vineyard Vines tie indeed lives up to the company's motto: "Don't be just another suit . . . tie on a vineyard vine."

R obert Charles is perhaps better known for the brand's leather belts than their ties. The belts are indeed lovely, each one handmade in the fair Italian city of Como. According to the brand, "Robert Charles belts are as much a delight to give as they are to receive." Fair enough.

A New Zealand brand, Robert Charles is inspired by Nature "at her boldest and vibrant best." Their ties are exquisite, it must be said—also handmade in Como, each pattern is inspired by the color and mood of the natural world. Their silk in particular is outstanding. Because the silk is washed and treated in two different countries before an image is printed onto it, the ties have a wonderful contrast between colors, as demonstrated here.

I believe that this tie was bought when I was lucky enough to spend time in the country filming Peter Jackson's *The Hobbit: The Desolation of Smaug*. While my character, the Master of Lake-town, was not particularly attractive (for the role I spent the entire time in a bald cap with a really bad comb-over wig on top, a wispy mustache and beard, and horrible blotchy skin and disgusting fingernails), New Zealand and this Robert Charles tie certainly are.

FRESH FROM NEW ZEALAND
MADE IN ITALY

robert charles

In 2018, after seventy years in the same location, Carroll & Co. of Beverly Hills closed its doors. A Hollywood sartorial institution, they were often heralded as the best in Los Angeles for traditional (some might say conservative) menswear. Certainly they had a loyal customer base of politicians, professionals, and celebrities—as well as plain old Stephen Fry. In the end, and as has so often been the case in expensive cities, the store's real estate became more valuable than the brand.

Carroll & Co. was started by Richard Carroll in the years following the Second World War. According to Ilse Metchek, who, as president of the California Fashion Association, knows about such things, "Before Carroll's, to be well dressed and well groomed, you either had to look like an Englishman or an Italian." Instead, the store offered a sleek sportswear aesthetic that right until the end carried an air of Hollywood panache. Richard Carroll worked as a publicist for Warner Bros. Fed up with having to drive downtown to Brooks Brothers to buy a suit, he solved the problem by starting his own brand. Always a dapper dresser, Carroll used his movie star contacts to good effect. Soon Fred Astaire, Clark Gable, and Cary Grant were all being outfitted at Carroll & Co.

It really was an institution. If Sinatra paid a visit to the store, someone would quickly ensure that only Sinatra music was playing. The famous violinist Jascha Heifetz would bring his violin with him and play during his fitting, so that his suits wouldn't feel tight during performances. Paul Newman once sent a note with the line "Fits terrific."

Rather fabulous, don't you think?

O zwald Boateng is one of the great names in British fashion. I have the honor of knowing him. We are what my Hungarian-Jewish grandfather would call *puszipajtás* (pronounced "pussy-pie-*tash*"). This splendid word signifies a "kissing friend." Hungarians are very demonstrative with their embraces; if you are *puszipajtás* with someone, it means you'd greet each other with a hug or a kiss if you met in the street.

Ozwald (who is not Hungarian, of course, but of Ghanaian descent) had the horrific job of dressing me for the first five or six BAFTA Film Award ceremonies that I hosted at the beginning of this century. I say "horrific job," because the Boateng style is very much one of elegant lines, of beautiful, almost teddy boy–length suit jackets, often in purples and teals. During exactly the time he was making me suits for these occasions, I was putting on the pounds at a rate of what seemed to be a stone a year. The poor chap must have felt like someone trying to stuff a beach ball into a bud vase. At least a necktie doesn't depend so much on waist size (although they can lie at a distressing horizontal on fat tummies). I am particularly fond of this tie—an artful play on the RAF roundel and the Union Flag.

Oswald designed clothes for *The Matrix*; *Lock, Stock and Two Smoking Barrels*; *Hannibal*; *Ocean's 13*; *Tomorrow Never Dies*; *Sex and the City*; and many others. A twenty-year retrospective at the Victoria & Albert Museum sixteen years ago confirmed his distinguished place in British fashion history. Fundamentally Savile Row, he trained under Tommy Nutter and, like his mentor, he manages always to be chic, elegant, and modern too. If he should ever get above himself, he can be forced to gaze upon a picture of me squeezed into one of his suitings. As P. G. Wodehouse put it, "He looked as if he had been poured into his clothes and had forgotten to say 'When!'"

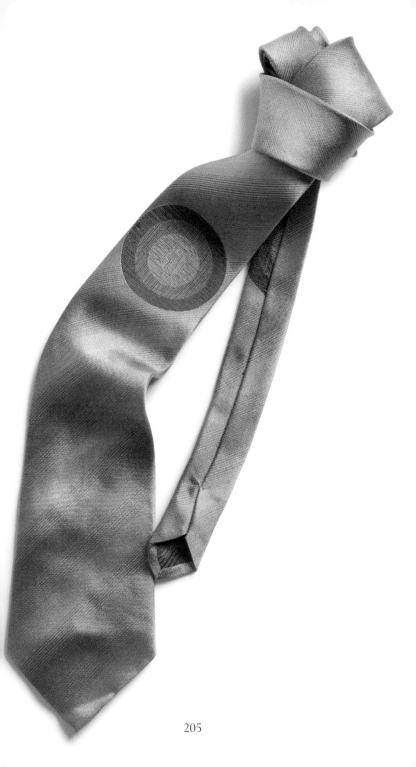

The last time I wore this tie, I was told that white ties were worn only by spivs. Some of you may be unfamiliar with this term—it's certainly not as common as it once was.

According to the illustrious institution that is the *Cambridge Dictionary*, a spiv is "a man, especially one who is well-dressed in a way that attracts attention, who makes money dishonestly." Here in the United Kingdom, the word likely originated on the racecourses and was certainly in common usage by the 1950s. Petty criminals dealing with black-market goods were the epitome of the spiv. The legendary actor and comedian Arthur English was famous for his portrayal of this lowlife ne'er-do-well; his spiv had a cockney accent and was always outrageously dressed, normally with a huge kipper tie.* In his stage show, English would unbutton his jacket to unfurl a dazzlingly flowered kipper tie ending around his knees. The tie had been made by his wife from curtain material. The accompanying joke, which always prompted great merriment, was that such a tie "keeps me knees warm in winter."

In truth, this tie has seen me through a number of daytime formal events, none of which—to the best of my knowledge—have involved the black market . . .

* Kipper ties have long been out of fashion. The craze started in 1966 and was (rightfully) over by 1979. The hallmark of the kipper tie was its width—up to six inches wide at the bottom.

R obert Talbott was a family-owned company for many years. It specializes in luxury handmade silk ties, priced accordingly. *This* example, however, is from their "Best of Class" line (you can see this written on the internal lining), and is, shall we say, much less expensive.

The company was founded after Robert and Audrey Talbott and their son, Robb, left the East Coast in 1950 and moved to Carmel, California. In her spare time, Audrey started sewing silk neckties for her husband and his friends. Recognizing his wife's talent, Robert turned her wares into a small business that specialized in luxury bow ties. After hand selling up and down the West Coast, the Talbotts opened their first shop in 1953. By 1969 the company was worth one million dollars.

The brand is currently up for sale—possibly due to the economic fallout of the pandemic, but also because Robert and Audrey's son, Robb Talbott, is focused on his winemaking. Wine and ties—now there's a winning combination.

P enrose London was started by Mitchell Jacobs, the man also behind the wonderful brand Duchamp. Indeed, there is a similarity of color and joie de vivre common to the ties of both. Jacobs founded Penrose in London's Soho district in 2008. Following his death in 2014, the company was bought by the Suffolk-based silk weavers Vanners, whose in-house ties also feature in *Fry's Ties*.

Born in Essex, Jacobs could recall having a suit made for him at the age of nine by his tailor grandfather, a Russian-Jewish émigré. A trip to Turnbull & Asser with his father in his teenage years was, according to Jacobs, "a Damascene moment for me. I was transfixed by the glorious colours and rich textures." Jacobs began working for many big names during the London menswear revolution of the '60s, including Tommy Nutter, Stanley Adams, and Jeff Kwintner. He then moved to New York to become a designer, where "an English accent and a sartorial cut of his jib got an enthusiastic young fella a long way back then."

Art-loving and jazz-loving, Penrose London was named after Roland Penrose, the British artist, historian, and poet who cofounded the Institute of Contemporary Arts. A passionate collector of modern art,

Roland Penrose used his artistic skills to train troops in camouflage during the Second World War, when the invasion of Britain seemed a very real threat. He authored the *Home Guard Manual for Camouflage*, copies of which can still be tracked down today.

I own at least a dozen Penrose London ties and shall continue to wear them whenever the day needs a bit of brightening up.

THE TRINITY KNOT

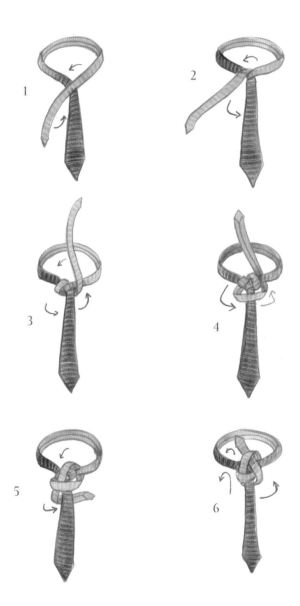

A h, Moss Bros. That beloved high-street institution that, as the United Kingdom's No. 1 formal menswear specialist, I would wager most men have worn at least once in their lifetime.

Moss Bros. has been "suiting the nation" since 1851. At the time that Charles Dickens started writing *Bleak House* and large crowds visited the Great Exhibition in Hyde Park, Moses Moss leased two small shops in a quiet corner of Covent Garden. Moses originally dealt in quality secondhand clothing. When, in 1894, he passed away, his sons Alfred and George inherited the business and moved the shop to nearby King Street. "Moss Bros." was proudly announced over the shop's door. In 1897 the store began hiring out suits for a fee of seven and sixpence (37.5p). Pre-pandemic, the modern Moss Bros. could hire out thousands of suits a week.

Perhaps less well-known nowadays is the Moss Bros. Military Department. Following the Boer War, "a collection of army oddments tucked away in a cupboard in the King Street store had little hope of finding homes," according to the Moss Bros. official history. But when, in 1910, a shop assistant named Martin dressed two officers in military frock coats, the Military Department was born. Newly commissioned officers in the First World War rushed to Covent Garden for their uniforms, while in the Second World War the company set up local outlets. The shop in Portsmouth, opened in 1940 to outfit the Navy, was particularly unlucky. It was struck within a few days of opening by the first bombs to hit the city. Company Secretary John Russell "was undeterred," and "found a wooden hut which he somehow persuaded the Navy to tow across the harbour." The hut stayed in business well into peacetime. A very British company indeed.

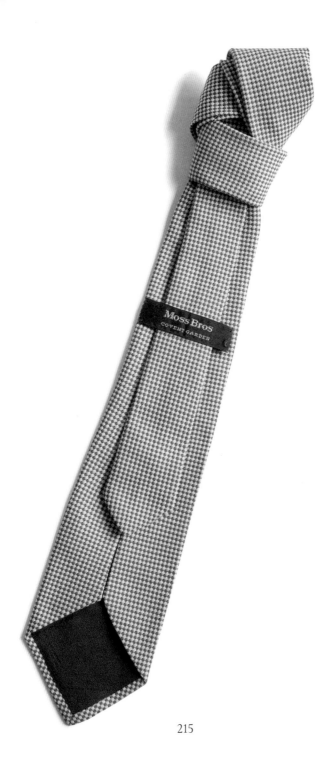

215

Thirty-one years ago I came to NORCAT (the Norfolk College of Arts and Technology) in King's Lynn to give a talk. An eager young photography student called Andy Gotts approached me and shyly but charmingly asked if I would stay on for an extra minute or so, so that he might photograph me. I obliged, and in ninety seconds he produced a few images, shown on pages 218–219.

Andy has since become one of the most desirable portrait photographers, especially of actors. He has been appointed an MBE by the Queen and won awards and recognition everywhere for his memorable and impressive work. And it all began with me. Talk about starting at the bottom and working your way up. And what should I be wearing in the pics but a Dunford Wood tie. It's almost unrecognizable in Andy's black-and-white shots, but it's unquestionably the same tie.

In the 1980s and early '90s, Hugh Dunford Wood was a name familiar to those of us who sought out unique and interesting ties. His hand-painted neckwear, cushions, and waistcoats were sold in Paul Smith and Harrods in the United Kingdom, in New York's Bergdorf Goodman and Saks Fifth Avenue, and in Yohji Yamamoto outlets in Tokyo.

I don't have the pleasure of knowing Hugh Dunford Wood, but I do know that he still creates charming and individual art and design pieces. He has a small studio that produces hand-painted wallpaper, and he makes murals on commission for factories, restaurants, hospitals, and private houses, as well as lino prints, etchings, paintings, sculpted steel, and all manner of choice artifacts. He no longer offers ties to the world, which may be a pity, but it does make this one—which was present for the debut of a wonderful portrait photographer—all the more special.

The simple playing card. So simple, that no one is quite certain where or when it originated. The Chinese have played *yezi ge*, or the "game of leaves," since the Tang dynasty of the ninth century AD. The first written mention of playing cards on the continent was by a German monk named Johannes in 1377. You might be fascinated to discover that the oldest complete deck of playing cards, the "Cloisters Deck," dates from the late fifteenth century, though there is also a near-complete set of cards from Mamluk Egypt, dating to some time around 1500, in Istanbul's Topkapı Palace Museum.

During one particularly exciting *QI* episode, I attempted something that had never been done, by any human being, since the *beginning* of time. And all I needed was a single pack of cards. A quick shuffle—I used the overhand, riffle, and weave techniques—and that was it. I had produced a pack of cards that had never before, in the history of our planet, been in that same order.

"What nonsense is this?" you might well say to yourself.

You see, it's a simple mathematical fact. The number of ways one can order fifty-two cards is a gigantic figure. It's a number known by mathematicians as "shriek"—you write it as "52!"—and it is 52 × 51 × 50 . . . all the way down to × 1. Which, when you get there, looks like: 80,658,175,170,943,878,571,660,636,856,403, 766,975,289,505,440,883,277,824,000,000,000,000.

This number is so big that were you to imagine if every star in our galaxy had a trillion planets, each with a trillion people living on them, and each of those people had a trillion packs of cards, and somehow they managed to shuffle all of them one thousand times per second—and they'd been doing that since the Big Bang—they would only *now* be starting to repeat shuffles.

So I can say, with all mathematical certainty, that my pack of cards had never before been in that order. It was, and remains, an absolute world first—something I cheerfully remember each time I wear this Nicole Miller tie.

H ot, bold colors, grand theatrical swagger, and unapologetic flair—no wonder Christian Marie Marc Lacroix was the favorite designer of *Ab Fab*'s Edina Monsoon. "It's Lacroix, sweetie!"

He had an unapologetic flair for losing money too. From its launch in 1987, through the 1990s and 2000s, the couture House of Lacroix never turned a profit. A €10 million loss in 2008 alone. Nonetheless, during this time he designed uniforms for Air France, brought out a copious line of fragrances, and created memorable costumes for operas and ballets. Private finance, and latterly the LVMH group (Louis Vuitton, Moët, Hennessy), more or less kept the company afloat and the *cher maître*'s rOtring pen flowing with new designs . . .

I n formal riding dress a cravat is often referred to as a "stock," although Americans call them "ascots." The word "cravat" itself has a most interesting derivation. It's a corruption of the word *Croat*, via the German *Krabate*, itself from Serbo-Croatian *Hrvat*. The Croats—or "Crabats," as they were called at the time—fought on the side of the Catholic League in the Thirty Years' War (1618–48: Eight million people died. It was a monstrous war, that one). The starched linen neckcloths that the Croat light cavalry favored were so associated with them that stocks, and subsequently most neckwear, became known as "cravats." Military clothing has quite a tradition of being taken up by civilians: The Wellington boot, raglan sleeve, and cardigan are all named after British army officers.

"Not more cricket!" I can hear you thinking to yourself. "Honestly, Stephen, how can you subject us to more sports ties . . ." Well, I think I may surprise some of you. The turquoise tie on the right was designed by T.M. Lewin and was first produced in 2013 for a joint awareness and fundraising day among the Lord's Taverners (the United Kingdom's leading youth cricket and disability sports charity), Chance to Shine (a national cricket charity), and the PCA (Professional Cricketers' Association) Benevolent Fund. Supporters on the day were encouraged to help turn the ground blue. The tie on the top of this page is the 2009 Npower Official ECB England v. Australia cricket tie, and the other tie—a Lord's Taverners cricket tie—is the less glamorous odd man out.

But you see, the story of the Ashes is actually a *love* story. In 1882, England lost a cricket match against Australia at the Oval. Their first defeat on home soil. In reaction to this, a mock obituary was published in *The Sporting Times*, saying that English cricket had *died* at the Oval. It would be cremated, and the ashes taken to

Australia. England's captain, the Hon. Ivo Bligh, made a vow that he would win the Ashes back and return them to England when they toured there that following winter. During the tour, Bligh's team played a friendly match at a country estate, which they won. At the end of that game, a woman named Florence Morphy took one of her perfume jars, filled it with the ashes of the burned bails—or so we believe—and presented it to Ivo Bligh as the Ashes of English Cricket, which he had set out to win back. Bligh returned victorious to England, and a year later set sail back to Australia, where he married Florence. There's been no love lost between England and Australia's cricket teams ever since.

I for one do truly believe that cricket, as first played by shepherds in the south of England, the game that spread to every corner of the world, the supreme bat-and-ball competition, the greatest game ever devised, will continue to provide unimagined pleasures. For, to misappropriate Benjamin Franklin, cricket is proof that God loves us and wants us to be happy.

THE FOUR-IN-HAND KNOT

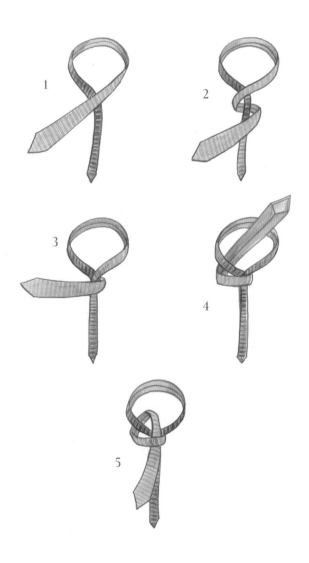

I can't recall when I bought this tie. There was an Old River apparel company in Canada, though they no longer seem to have stores in Montreal or Quebec. There is still an Old River in Palermo, where, according to their website, "you will find, in our historic store in Via Giuseppe Sciuti, 27, all the fabrics, clothing, and accessories that have made our history and made the man who dresses Old River unique and original with his timeless British Style for thirty years." ·I have no idea if the two companies were related, but the tie's logo of three men in a boat (perhaps a kayak?), with oars raised, suggests that this fine specimen of neckwear is indeed from Sicily, as the logo also appears on the company's Facebook page.

Did I perhaps take a stroll down the Via Giuseppe Sciuti, and was my eye caught by a particularly fetching window display? I'm afraid such knowledge has been lost to history. Regardless of origin, I do think that this tie, with its mix of paisley and pattern, carries a certain charm. Whether it is a particularly British charm I leave to you, dear reader.

231

"KNOW, FIRST, WHO YOU ARE, AND THEN ADORN YOURSELF ACCORDINGLY."

Epictetus

At some point I had to present you with this zigzag Armani tie. You can see how loved it is by the dilapidated state of the fat end. Used for polishing spectacles and collecting dropped food, the poor thing looks ready to curl up and die. Which is a shame, because this snazzy design speaks to my very depths. It might remind you of the Royal Artillery regimental tie, which has similar jagged red lines, but with sharper and acuter angles, I think. Also, that tie is on a field of midnight blue, rather than this offering's mushroomy beige.

In the 1980s Giorgio Armani became the hippest, hottest, and happeningest of all the designers in the world. It was the era of "unstructured" jackets, raglan sleeves, linen shirts, and spacious trousers for men, and of big hair and padded shoulders for women. Eric Clapton, fresh from rehab, popularized the tasteful, subdued, and loose-fitting Armani look. Emporio Armani, Armani Jeans, Armani Junior, Armani sunglasses, Armani loafers, Armani bags, Armani hotels—contributing to the man's substantial net worth, said to be north of eight billion of your Earth dollars.

I think it's true to say that this tie is the only Armani object I've ever owned. Not out of dislike for the brand, but because the company doesn't really offer the kind of clobber that's made for the likes of me. Armani looks fine on other people. Snake-hipped and wasp-waisted types look especially good in it, but it just won't sit right on Stephens. Which is perfectly okay by me, so long as I have this dear old tie.

Many Britons, Londoners especially, disdain Harrods these days. Partly because the store is so popular with tourists, partly because of a disenchantment that grew in the 1970s. An influx of extraordinarily wealthy Arabs shopping there gave rise to a casual (and unattractive) xenophobia. The British economy was in tatters, inflation rampant, and the prospect of native-born Britons being able to afford to go there seemed remote. Then an ugly fight for ownership was won by Mohamed Al-Fayed, and what had been thought of as the Grand Old Lady of Knightsbridge, a comfortable, prosperous—expensive, certainly—but unshowy institution, seemed to have become just another rich man's counter, another token property in the ostentatious game of Monopoly that billionaires play. And now, of course, it is owned by Qatar's sovereign wealth fund, and it looks like just another high-priced mall.

Remnants of Harrods's former grandeur linger in the magnificent food halls—the fish fountain is still spectacular, for example. The glory has not so much faded as been spray-painted in bright gold. "Oh, I haven't been to Horrids for ages . . .," you'll hear people say in a distastefully snobbish way. Despite the awful own-brand teddy bears and red buses, and all the flashiness, I am secretly still quite bewitched by the place. The green uniforms on the wonderful doormen, the old escalators (Britain's very, very first was Harrods's "moving staircase" in 1898), those food halls: "Meet you at the HJB at Roddy's," the trendy would say in the '60s (meaning the Health Juice Bar). When young I always got a frisson walking through the menswear department. My gay friends and I would vie with each other to see if any of us could get the glad eye from the large contingent of gay men who worked there. Oh, the winks and grins. Such moments were a thrill back in the dark days of repressive laws and unkindly attitudes.

Harrods still labels its own lines. But I can't remember when I got this particular offering. Maybe a long time ago from an assistant I thought charming . . . Who knows? This tie may be nothing remarkable, perhaps, but it's nothing to be ashamed of either. Highly wearable, in fact. Good old Horrids.

make no secret of my affection for knitted ties. Comfortable and stylish, they really are the best of both. But you might say that these Huntsman ties have something a little *extra*. They are, as the Huntsman website proclaims, "the most exquisite garments money can buy & the human hand can make." Well then.

Huntsman was the inspiration for the spy agency–*cum*–Savile Row shop Kingsman, in the spy comedy film directed by Matthew Vaughn. No. 126 New Bond Street was the site of the first shop in 1809, though it was originally a "gaiter and breeches maker." The tailor Henry Huntsman bought the shop in 1849 and swiftly moved its location to London's Albermarle Street while also renaming the business. Huntsman became well known for dressing the hunting and riding aristocracy, even receiving a Royal Warrant for "Leather Breeches Maker," first to HRH The Prince of Wales (later Edward VII), then to Queen Victoria's second son Prince Alfred, Duke of Saxe Coburg Gotha, and finally to Queen Victoria herself in 1888. Like so many menswear outfitters, Huntsman supplied the military during the wars. The shop moved to 11 Savile Row in 1919, where it remains today. Throughout the twentieth century Hollywood took notice, and Clark Gable, David Niven, Rex Harrison, Laurence Olivier,

Paul Newman, Dirk Bogarde, Katharine Hepburn, and Gregory Peck were all dressed by Huntsman.

Curiously, in 1921 a customer left two stags' heads in the shop ahead of what one presumes was a long, perhaps even louche, lunch. He never returned to collect them, and they now hang over the shop's fireplace.

S *prezzatura*. A term first used in Castiglione's 1528 *The Book of the Courtier*, it means "a certain nonchalance, so as to conceal all art and make whatever one does or says appear to be without effort and almost without any thought about it." Or, according to the Harrods website, "that breed of relaxed elegance unique to Romans."

The Italian house of Brioni is a master of tailoring, evoking a sophisticated, jet-set lifestyle. *Sprezzatura*, if you will. Yet I think I'm right in saying that Brioni is not necessarily a household name, despite making history in 1952 by hosting the world's first men's catwalk in Florence's Palazzo Pitti. A Brioni suit is a thing of true beauty—it's purported to take twenty-four hours to make just one (the House has a precise 220-step method that requires seven thousand handmade hidden stitches). Brioni also carries the distinction of being the only label to train tailors at its own school, the Scuola di Alta Sartoria. Established in 1985, the school selects sixteen students every four years. There is, as the legend goes, a particular "Roman style" of tailoring passed down from master to apprentice there in the wooded hills of Abruzzo, a region east of Rome best known in the United Kingdom, I imagine, for its Montepulciano d'Abruzzo wine.

Brioni's Chief Master Tailor, Angelo Petrucci, who became an apprentice at the age of thirteen, maintains that "you need to start before the age of twenty, otherwise your hands will not be sensitive enough to have a feeling for the cloth."

Brioni was founded in the heart of Rome, on Via Barberini 79, by Nazareno Fonticoli, a master tailor, and his business partner Gaetano Savini in 1945. They have a smart store in London, on Mayfair's Bruton Street. Worn by James Bond and John Wayne on the silver screen and by Brad Pitt (a Brioni House

Ambassador), Barack Obama, and Nelson Mandela in real life, my small slice of Brioni, this tie, is indeed a thing of beauty.

Yves Saint Laurent had the spectacled look (also favored by the other great Yves, Yves Montand), which on men of any other nationality can look dull and nerdy, but which the French somehow manage to make impossibly glamorous.

Yves Saint Laurent was born in Oran (the Algerian coastal city in which Camus set the plague in his now horribly pertinent novel *La Peste*). At a young age, YSL caught the attention of that giant of French couture, Christian Dior, who mentored and encouraged him. After Dior's sudden fatal heart attack in 1957, YSL was made head of the House of Dior. He was just twenty-one years old, chief designer of the most celebrated and influential fashion enterprise in the world.

YSL's big leap was in making prêt-à-porter—ready-to-wear—as chic and desirable as his couture lines. More so, perhaps. A blizzard of fragrances, aftershaves, and accessories increased his prevalence and huge financial success. Unlike, say, Pierre Cardin, he did not seem to cheapen and devalue his brand by over-expansion. For my part, this is a tie I still wear with pleasure.

P aul Stuart is another American clothing brand promising "classic menswear" and "expert craftsmanship." The brand's style has been described as a "blend of Savile Row, Connecticut living, and the concrete canyons of New York." Hmm. Whether or not this makes sense to you, I'm sure you'll agree that this is indeed quite a smart-looking tie.

Paul Stuart was founded in 1938 by the haberdasher Mr. Ralph Ostrove. Ralph named the company after his son, Paul Stuart Ostrove, and set up shop in Manhattan's Midtown, at the corner of Madison Avenue and 45th Street. The company has remained there ever since, surviving the economic and cultural tribulations of war, economic disruptions, and changing winds of fashion. Cary Grant wore Paul Stuart in Hitchcock's *North by Northwest*, and this old Hollywood sensibility imbues the brand today; the sartorial destination MR PORTER defines Paul Stuart as "drawing inspiration from the sophisticated designs of the 1920s through to early 1960s."

The Paul Stuart logo consists of Dink Stover sitting on the Yale fence. I'm not sure many of us remember who Dink Stover was—in the logo he's wearing brogues, a flat cap, and a three-piece suit. Dink is the titular character of Owen Johnson's novel *Stover at Yale*, which tells the story of undergraduate life at Yale at the turn of the twentieth century. I suppose this explains the "Connecticut living"?

245

I suspect the C&A brand does not have a home in many wardrobes. Perhaps it does? It's a diffusion label from the Belgian-German-Dutch C&A, a chain of "fast-fashion" retail stores. The brothers Clemens and August Brenninkmeijer founded the company in 1841 as a Dutch textile company, using their initials to form the company name.

C&A used to be visible throughout many towns in Britain, but steady competition from the likes of Tesco and Asda's own clothing brands, as well as high-street shops such as Zara and H&M, meant that in 2000 C&A withdrew from Britain. There are still many shops throughout Europe, you'll be relieved to know.

This is not a particularly luxurious tie, with its 100 percent polyester composition. And yet I am fond of its combination of paisley with a rural cottage landscape, complete with a picture frame. I still wear it with great affection.

247

ercy Bysshe Shelley's verse play *The Cenci* is a daring story of incest and murder, one that has been strikingly reimagined by the great and mad Antonin Artaud, amongst others. But Davide Cenci (pronounced "Tchen-tchi")—while possibly related to the Cenci dynasty that so disgraced itself in the sixteenth century—has committed no crimes that I know of, except perhaps one against language. See if you can make sense of what the website for the company named after him says:

> In providing comfort for our customers, we have also learned not to be too comfortable with ourselves. Since we have found, after time, that the road we travel on is a road of discovery and that the arrival point is so desired initially is not a point we will ever reach nor want to.

I managed the first sentence without too much trouble, but I will puzzle over that last one for eternity. It sounds like babble from the sickbed, though perhaps I'm missing something.

Shush, Stephen. All companies, whether they're in fashion, furnishings, or finance, inflict mad and meaningless mission statements on the world. It's just something we have to put up with. Fortunately we can say that—the above aberration aside—Davide Cenci has nothing to be ashamed of. They've been selling well-designed and well-made items to men and women in Rome, Milan, and New York since 1926. The Cenci New York store is on the Upper East Side, just a couple of blocks from where I had my apartment on Madison and 77th Street in the naughty '90s. Fond memories.

This particular tie offering might not stand out from the crowd, yet its understated style and quality charm well enough. One of the great things about ties, of course, is that you don't have to try them on for size. Even socks might not fit by the time you get them home. A tie is a straightforward purchase that can be based entirely on color, pattern, and form. And if, like me, you are pretty much embarrassed by your body and how clothes look on you compared to the perfect models and Adonises whose images pervade our world, then a good tie can allow the little surge of self-confidence that makes all the difference.

Shanghai Tang was a clothing label founded by Sir David Tang, "the Hong Kong–born billionaire bon viveur known worldwide for his legendary parties," according to *Condé Nast Traveller*, which in 2017 proclaimed Tang one of their "50 Best Travellers of Our Time." (The Condé Nast list included everyone from the Dalai Lama to the Beckhams.) This tie perfectly embodies David's design sensibilities. Just the right side of kitsch, with a Shanghai scene still colonial in atmosphere.

Tang was a dear friend. The first time I met him I thought him pugnacious—socially pugilistic almost. "Bullshit. Nonsense. Bollocks. Rubbish." All in response to a mild comment on the weather. Born rich. A gambler capable of losing £250,000 in one night. A collector of people. A fixture at all the smart aristocrat shoots. A world of private jets, yachts, and clubs. Apoplectically rude to staff. He never left home without his Egyptian cotton pajamas by French brand Charvet embroidered with "DT sleeping." So far I have described a horror of obnoxious entitlement and high-end loutishness. But . . . how deceptive.

A deep, almost bottomless well of kindness lay under all that strange surface nonsense. He would do anything, it seemed, to hide the full, open warmth of a soft and generous heart. If you had a birthday, published a book, had been away for three months, got engaged, had been trashed in the public prints, won an award, or broken an arm, David would use it as a pretext for holding a dinner in your honor. I loved the man dearly.

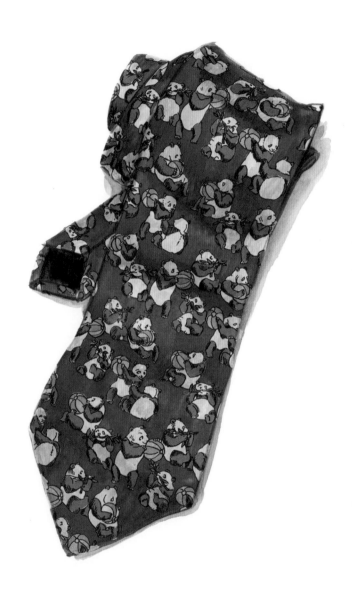

This may surprise you, but pandas have twice come into my life. In 2009, I voiced a "languorous panda" for the comedy sketch show *A Walk on the Wild Side*. My panda was overburdened due to the fact that it was the world's only *celebrity* panda. I noticed, quite rightly, that the bear community has any number of well-known members: Paddington, Pudsey, Pooh . . . Yet can anyone name a well-known panda? Indeed not. (I refused to acknowledge Po, the Kung Fu Panda. Pandas abhor violence and wouldn't know nunchucks from a clarinet.)

In 2014, the kind folks at the World Wildlife Fund passed me a panda, as part of their #passthepanda challenge ahead of the WWF's annual Earth Hour. Earth Hour, for those of you who don't know, occurs during the last weekend in March. Everyone, across the globe, is invited to turn off any nonessential lights for one hour to show a communal concern for the future of our planet.

This panda tie, by Pink, shows the delightful scene of the creature being entertained by a ball—I'm not sure if it's a beach ball or some other sort. I do know that the giant panda is gravely threatened by climate change. Let's hope that we're able to change our ways and continue to be enchanted by these animals in real life, rather than on ties alone.

From pandas to pigs, it would seem. And unlike the former, history is full of many famous pigs. Peppa Pig, Wilbur the pig (friend to Charlotte, in E. B. White's classic *Charlotte's Web*), Pumbaa (technically a warthog, but I think he counts), Porky Pig, Spider-Pig, Miss Piggy, and, of course, Napoleon, a "fierce-looking" Berkshire boar and the leader of the revolt in George Orwell's *Animal Farm*.

Using the allegory of a Sussex small-holding, Orwell (whose real name was Eric Arthur Blair) wrote to expose the betrayals, barbarities, and distortions of Stalin. After fighting against Franco's fascists in the Spanish Civil War in his thirties, Orwell had seen firsthand the lies, cruelty, and ruthless suppression of free thinking employed by the Soviets. But at just the time Orwell was formulating this story, in the early 1940s, the Soviet Union was hurling herself against the might of Hitler's Wehrmacht in the most attritional act of sacrificial homeland defense the world had ever seen. By doing so, she was turning the tide of the entire war, allowing Britain and her allies some cover with which to prepare for D-Day and the invasion of France. Without Stalin and his totalitarian grip on the vast millions of citizens he controlled, there is no chance the Nazi threat could ever have been overcome. Many of Orwell's friends thought that for him to attack the Soviet Union at this time was folly, or worse. It is not altogether surprising that Orwell found it hard to get his novella published, and it was not until after victory in Europe that *Animal Farm* finally found a publisher. Seven or eight years later, the Americans were dropping copies behind the Iron Curtain from balloons.

Now, the jolly pigs on my New & Lingwood tie are not in any way associated with Snowball, Napoleon, and Squealer, the pigs from Orwell's text. And yet, I can't wear this tie without thinking, even fleetingly, of Orwell's closing line: "The creatures outside looked from pig to man, and from man to pig, and from pig to man again; but already it was impossible to say which was which."

This wonderfully jazzy tie is made by Van Buck England, a brand based in Sible Hedingham, Essex. Three men—Peter Rayner, Ivan Palmer, and Tim Buckman—founded the company in 1976. I can see how "van" and "buck" became part of the brand name, though I'm at a loss to see how Peter Rayner fits in? Anyhoo, today Van Buck England is a second-generation family business with "over 100,000 ties, bow ties, cravats, cummerbunds, pocket squares, hankies and cuff links in stock." Their website showcases a client list including Jon Snow, Ian Hislop, David Cameron, John Bercow, Sir Ian Botham, and, errrrr, Stephen Fry.

Many Van Buck ties are made in "limited edition" runs of one hundred—this one is from a few years ago. It combines two of my favorite tie motifs: the classic paisley teardrop and flowers—let's call these daisies. The colors are undeniably bold, all iridescent turquoise and purple.

One last word on the bohemian teardrop. Paisley, having traveled the silk routes from East to West, adorned everything from luxury shawls in the nineteenth century to Oscar Wilde's silk paisley smoking jacket and cravat. The pattern was popular on the bandanas favored by the Beatles, the Rolling Stones, Jimi Hendrix, and The Who, and was equally fashionable with the "hippie" culture of the same era. Might there be something vaguely psychedelic about this tie?

B enson & Clegg pride themselves on being the only "true bespoke tailors situated in the St. James's district." Located at 9 Piccadilly Arcade, Jermyn Street, they hold the Royal Warrant to HRH The Prince of Wales as suppliers of buttons, badges, and military neckwear.

The company was founded in 1937 by Mr. Harry Benson and Mr. Thomas Clegg, both of whom had been working for Hawes & Curtis for many years. Benson and Clegg felt that they could bring something different to the sartorial scene—a style of tailoring unique to them. Benson in particular was ground-breaking in his design and development of the backless evening dress waistcoat. Not such a wardrobe essential nowadays, I agree.

There is a strong royal connection to the brand. Prince Albert, Duke of York, was a famous customer even before he became His Majesty King George VI. The king continued to frequent Benson & Clegg, recognizing the brand as his tailor in 1944 with a Royal Warrant.

Over the years B&C have almost become more famous for their accessories: their ties, buttons, badges, and cuff links. In 1973 Benson & Clegg supplied a Royal Navy tie to the James Bond production *Live and Let Die*, and B&C accessories have also appeared in *Peaky Blinders* and *The Crown*. As well as around the neck of Mr. Stephen Fry.

IMAGE CREDITS

TRADEMARKS

Abercrombie & Fitch is a registered trademark of Abercrombie & Fitch Trading Co. Adidas is a registered trademark of Adidas AG Joint Stock Company. Amazon is a registered trademark of Amazon Technologies, Inc.

Apple is a registered trademark of Apple Inc. Armani is a registered trademark of Giorgio Armani S.p.A. Armani Junior is a registered trademark of Giorgio Armani S.p.A. Arpège is a registered trademark of Interparfums Suisse SÀRL. Astley's is a registered trademark of William Astley & Co. Ltd. Aston Martin is a registered trademark

of Aston Martin Lagonda Ltd. BAFTA is a registered trademark of British Academy of Film and Television Arts. Bergdorf Goodman is a registered trademark of NM Nevada Trust Corporation. Big Mac is a registered trademark of McDonald's Corporation. Birkin is a registered trademark of Hermès International SCA.

Boden is a registered trademark of J. P. Boden & Co. Ltd. Brioni is a registered trademark of Brioni S.p.A.

Brooks Brothers is a registered trademark of BB IPCO LLC. C&A is a registered trademark of C&A AG Corporation. Calvin Klein is a registered trademark of The Trustee of the Calvin Klein Trademark Trust. Canali is a registered trademark of Canali Ireland Ltd. LLC. Charles Tyrwhitt is a registered trademark of Charles Tyrwhitt

Shirts Ltd. Charvet is a registered trademark of Charvet Place Vendôme S.A. Christian Dior is a registered trademark of Christian Dior Couture, S.A. Christian

Lacroix is a registered trademark of Christian Lacroix, SNC Magend Holdings, LLC. Coca-Cola is a registered trademark of The Coca-Cola Company. Davidoff is a registered trademark of Davidoff & Cie SA. Davide Cenci

is a registered trademark of Davide Cenci & Figli S.R.L. DÉCLIC is a registered trademark of Les Grands Chais de France SAS. Disney is a registered trademark of

Disney Enterprises, Inc. Doc Martens is a registered trademark of
Dr. Martens International Trading GmbH. Duchamp is a registered
trademark of Roffe Accessories, Inc. Dunhill is a registered
trademark of Alfred Dunhill
Ltd. Corporation. eBay is a registered trademark of eBay Inc.
Emporio Armani is a registered trademark of Giorgio Armani S.p.A.
Ercol is a registered trademark of Ercol Furniture Ltd. Ermenegildo
Zegna is a registered trademark of Ermenegildo Zegna
Corporation. Etro is a registered trademark of Etro S.p.A. Facebook
is a registered trademark of Meta Platforms, Inc. Ferrari is a
registered trademark of Ferrari S.p.A. Fisher-Price is a registered
trademark of Mattel, Inc. Fornasetti is a registered trademark of
Immaginazione S.R.L. LLC. Fortnum & Mason is a registered
trademark of Fortnum & Mason PLC. Geo. F. Trumper is a
registered trademark of Geo. F. Trumper (Perfumer & Products)
Ltd. Google is a registered trademark of Google LLC. H&M is a
registered trademark of H & M Hennes & Mauritz AB. Hackett is a
registered trademark of Hackett Ltd. LLC. Hallmark is a registered
trademark of Hallmark Licensing, LLC. Harris Tweed is a registered
trademark of Harris Tweed Authority. Harrods is a registered
trademark
of Harrods Corporate Management Ltd. Company. Harvey Nichols
is a registered trademark of Harvey Nichols and Company
Ltd. Harvie & Hudson is a registered trademark of Harvie and
Hudson Ltd. Hawes & Curtis is a registered trademark of Hawes &
Curtis Ltd. PLC. Hermès is a registered trademark of Hermès
International SCA. Hogwarts is a registered trademark of Warner
Bros. Entertainment Inc. Hublot is a registered trademark of Hublot
SA. IBM is a registered trademark of International Business
Machines Corporation. Instagram is a
registered trademark of Instagram LLC. E-Type is
a registered trademark of Jaguar Land Rover Ltd. Jean
Paul Gaultier is a registered trademark of Puig France. Kelly is a
registered trademark of Hermès International SCA. Lamborghini
is a registered trademark of Automobili Lamborghini S.p.A. Lanvin
is a registered trademark of Jeanne Lanvin Joint Stock Company.
L.L.Bean is a registered trademark of L.L. Bean, Inc. Louis Vuitton
is a registered trademark of Louis Vuitton Malletier SAS. LVMH is
a registered trademark of LVMH Moët Hennessy Louis Vuitton

Company. Lycra is a registered trademark
of The Lycra Company LLC. Mac is a registered
trademark of Apple Inc. Marks & Spencer is a registered
trademark of Marks and Spencer PLC. Maserati is a registered
trademark of Maserati S.p.A. Mickey Mouse
is a registered trademark of Disney Enterprises, Inc. Microsoft is
a registered trademark of Microsoft Corporation. Missoni is a
registered trademark of Missoni S.P.A. Monopoly is a registered
trademark of Hasbro, Inc. Moschino is a registered trademark of
Moschino S.p.A. Mothercare is a registered trademark of
Mothercare UK Ltd. Museum Artifacts is a registered trademark of
Sourcing Network International, LLC. New & Lingwood is
a registered trademark of New and Lingwood Ltd. Nicole Miller is
a registered trademark of Kobra International,
Ltd. Obsession is a registered trademark of Calvin Klein Cosmetic
Corporation. Old River is a registered trademark of Jcorp Inc. Paul
Smith is a registered trademark of Paul Smith Group Holdings Ltd.
Paul Stuart is a registered trademark of Paul Stuart, Inc. Penrose
London is a registered trademark of Silk Industries Ltd. LPC. Per
Una
is a registered trademark of Marks and Spencer PLC. Pierre
Cardin is a registered trademark of Cardin, Pierre. Polo Ralph
Lauren is a registered trademark of PRL USA Holdings, Inc. Racing
Green is a registered trademark of Baird Group Ltd. Ralph Lauren is
a registered trademark
of PRL USA Holdings, Inc. Reiss is a registered trademark of Reiss
Ltd. Robert Talbott is a registered trademark of
RT Brands LLC. rOtring is a registered trademark of Luxembourg
Brands SARL. Rubik's Cube is a registered trademark of Spin
Master Toys UK Ltd. PLC. Saks Fifth Avenue is a registered
trademark of SAKS.COM LLC. Shanghai Tang is a registered
trademark of Tangs Department Ltd. Simon Carter is a registered
trademark of Simon Carter Ltd. Snapchat is a registered trademark
of Snapchat, Inc. Tesco is a registered trademark of Tesco Stores
Ltd. Tintin is a registered trademark of Moulinsart S.A. TikTok is a
registered trademark of Bytedance Ltd. T.M. Lewin is a registered
trademark of T.M. Lewin & Sons Ltd. Tommy Hilfiger is a registered
trademark of Tommy Hilfiger Licensing LLC. Turnbull & Asser is a
registered trademark